Walking Dreams

SALVATORE
FERRAGAMO
1898 - 1960

Catalogue Coordination
Stefania Ricci

Design
GALERA / José Luis Lugo

Shoe Photographs
Stefano Biliotti
Christopher Broabent
Roberto Quagli

Copy Editing
María Teresa González

Translation
Gregory Dechant
Sandra Luna

Publication Assistant
Isabel Garcés

The Museo del Palacio de Bellas Artes would like to thank Wanda
Miletti Ferragamo, president of Salvatore Ferragamo Italia s.p.a.,
for the loan of material from the Museo Salvatore Ferragamo.

First edition 2006
© Salvatore Ferragamo Italia s.p.a.
© Editorial RM, S.A. de C.V.
© Editorial RM Verlag, S.L.

© Texts
  Margo Glantz
  Mercedes Iturbe
  Stefania Ricci
  Alberto Ruy Sánchez

© Images
  Alinari Archive, Florence
  Corbis/Grazia Neri Archive, Milan
  State Archives, Rome
  Salvatore Ferragamo Archive, Florence
  AFE, Historical Archive of Cinema, Rome
  Locchi Historical Archive, Florence
  The Academy of Motion Picture Arts and Sciences, Los Angeles
  Experimental Center of Cinematography, Rome
  Phototeque, New York
  Time Life, New York

ISBN Editorial RM: 968-5208-63-8
ISBN Editorial RM Verlag: 84-934426-3-1
Depósito legal: M-11.508-2006

Distributed in the USA and Canada by D.A.P.
155 Sixth Avenue. 2nd Floor
New York, NY 10013
www.artbook.com
Tel: 212-627-1999
Toll free fax: 800-478-3128

Walking Dreams

SALVATORE FERRAGAMO
1898 - 1960

SALVATORE FERRAGAMO ∎ MUSEO DEL PALACIO DE BELLAS ARTES ∎ EDITORIAL RM

CONTENTS

PREFACE

Wanda Miletti Ferragamo

I am extremely proud to present, for the first time in Mexico and in the prestigious Museum of the Palacio de Bellas Artes, the work of my husband Salvatore: the most outstanding of the designs he created in the course of his career, from the museum that bears his name in Florence.

This is an important occasion, and one that I hope will be a stimulus and an inspiration to all, especially to young people, wherever they may be, who are always in need of positive examples.

The story of my husband Salvatore is an extraordinary one, and typically Italian, though it also has an innovate American dimension. The United States constituted a formative experience for Salvatore, and left a profound mark on him, teaching him that everything is possible, so long as one looks to the future and is willing to dream. Although I lived with him for so many years, I am still amazed by how much he was able to achieve, so rapidly and in spite of his humble origins.

But his life cannot be explained only in terms of his talent and his creativity, however exceptional, as this book and this exhibition demonstrate. Many were the underlying causes of his success; many were the forces that spurred him on: the perfectionism of the artisan, who refuses to accept less than a job well done; the passion for his trade, a dedication that transformed a craft into an art, however humble the work; and his foresight.

He was a man, moreover, who never gave himself airs. Although he was a titan, there was not a trace of arrogance in his character, and still less of megalomania: quite the contrary. His attitude toward life was one of intense generosity. He was also generous to himself, to his ideas, projects, and dreams. He gave himself wholly to whatever he was doing, often, in truth, without considering the costs and the risks... He possessed that optimism that goes along with talent and willpower. And above all he had a big heart, which guided him in both his work and his private life.

His humanity, his ability to feel an emotion and transmit it to others, is present in his work. It is what makes his shoes unique and eternal.

Salvatore Ferragamo looking through the vinyl sole of one of his famous shoes, created in the late 50's, 1955. Photo Locchi. Locchi Historical Archive, Florence.

Left endpaper:
Lucio Venna, advertising design for Ferragamo, 1930. Museo Salvatore Ferragamo, Florence.

Page 4:
Salvatore Ferragamo controlling the work of his shoemakers in the late 1930's. Photo David Lees. Salvatore Ferragamo Archive, Florence.

WALKING DREAMS

Mercedes Iturbe

In the history of humanity, shoes —especially women's shoes— have played a singular role. Beyond simply protecting the feet and making it easier to walk, they have been the source of dreams, fantasies, sensuality, and eroticism. A woman's beautiful feet are still more provocative and exciting when covered or partly covered by a pair of fine shoes. Women's shoes have been a permanent fetish in art, cinema, and literature. One has only recall various of the films of Luis Buñuel, in which the powerful presence of a shoe protecting a woman's foot elicits irrepressible reactions of sensuality, transformed at times into jealousy or lust.

The beauty of a naked woman's legs is accentuated by shoes, and her figure in general is rendered more voluptuous and desirable. It is easy to see why striptease artists the world over, of whatever category, keep their high heels on even when they have rid themselves of the rest of their clothing. And most men's magazines featuring nude or scantily-clad women heighten the sensuality of their models' bodies with shoes that not only emphasize the beauty of the legs, but of all those provocative feminine curves.

For many men, women's shoes are a fetish object, and for some women, in addition to being a coveted commodity, they are a weapon of seduction. Women love the possibilities offered by shoes, even to the absurd extreme of enduring those that make their feet ache. Unconcerned by questions of comfort, they like the way they look on their feet.

Even as a child, I had inherited my mother's fascination with shoes. When I was a little girl I would always accompany her on her shopping trips to the department stores in El Paso, Texas, where we went once a year to visit my maternal grandparents. The experience of seeing a large number of shoes spread out over a carpeted floor, ready to caress and to outline, one by one, the feet of each customer, was more exciting to me than any game. As a teenager I would often wear my mother's shoes, sometimes with her permission and sometimes without. I might add that her feet were smaller than mine, so wearing her shoes could be a minor torture at times, which I endured for the sake of having them on my feet.

Salvatore Ferragamo with his models wearing the new invention: the 'kimo', 1951. Photo David Lees. Salvatore Ferragamo Archive, Florence.

Salvatore Ferragamo with Joan Crawford in the Hollywood Boot Shop, 1926. Photo Alinari. Alinari Archive, Florence.

"D.W. Griffith –Ferragamo writes– early in my career suggested that I run a beauty competition for the best feet, ankles and legs in the city. He would offer the first prize –a six months' film contract– and I could give second and third prize of shoes. The event was organized and the winner, according to the panel of judges, was a girl named Marjorie Howard. My only choice was a girl with beautiful legs who was trying hard to break in to films. Her name was Joan Crawford. I forget whether she won second or third prize; but I know that those were the first shoes of mine she ever wore, and she is my customer still".

When I received the proposal to mount an exhibition of shoes by Salvatore Ferragamo, I was didn't know anything about his life and or about the museum devoted to him in Florence. All I knew were those marvelous display windows with shoes flying about in the Ferragamo stores in many cities of the world. Quality and beauty sustained by the magnificent presence of an exuberant imagination.

On analyzing the proposal, I realized it involved a show that surpassed the world of fashion and formed an undeniable part of the universe of creation: tiny hand-made sculptures executed with daring and passion at the service of the beauty and the care of women's feet. The wooden lasts fashioned by Ferragamo after he took the measurements of his clients' feet were another kind of magnificent sculpture, not only serving the manufacture of shoes, but also concealing anatomical secrets, seeking beauty, and drawing an enigmatic map of pleasures and obsessions.

Together with the material of the exhibition, presented previously in other versions in prestigious museums in Europe, Asia, and the United States, I received information about Salvatore Ferragamo himself, his biography and other documents that describe his early and decided vocation as a shoemaker.

Short in stature, Ferragamo was the eleventh child of poor parents from a village near Naples called Bonito. The very name of his native village, for those who speak Spanish, forms part of the magic of a life of perseverance, conviction, and sacrifice on a clearly defined path.

When still very young, and without giving it too much thought, Ferragamo decided to emigrate to the United States, where several of his brothers had already gone. Suddenly, through these family connections, he found his way into the world of motion pictures, which presented him with immediate challenges and goals. Within a few years Salvatore Ferragamo had become the shoemaker of celebrities. The most famous actors and actresses of Hollywood were seduced by the personality and talent of the artist, and became his faithful clients. His rise to fame was meteoric, but this was not enough for him, and he decided to improve his qualifications. He studied comparative anatomy, physics, chemistry, and mathematics at the University of Los Angeles. He was concerned not only with the beauty, but also with the care, of the feet and the body in all their aspects.

At the age of 28, having quickly gained unexpected success and a thorough knowledge of his greatest obsession –the human foot–, he made the decision to return to his own country. He did not believe the quality of Italian craft would ever be equaled in the United States, where mass production was diametrically opposed to the goal of a hand-made shoe. Ferragamo chose to settle in Florence, and not by chance: he was conscious of the impact of the city's reputation in the world, thanks to the magnificence of its art and its long tradition of high-quality crafts.

Ferragamo was a man of his time, with the profound vision of a creator. This allowed him to combine innovation and tradition, functionality and technological experimentation, exuberance and comfort, in his work.

Never subject to the dictates of fashion, he himself went much farther. He assimilated the great contributions of art and architecture that made an impression on him in different cities of the world and translated them into the innovative daring of his designs.

The hard times of the war years and post-war period and a certain leaning toward simple materials led him to use nylon and cellophane wrap to create shoes that had never before been imagined in the world of design. This made him at once a revolutionary and a classic designer, who gained absolute fame in the world of international fashion.

Ferragamo devoted his life to the human foot, that extremity of our lower limbs that hold us upright on the ground. The arch of the foot is nothing less than the support of the weight of our bodies and what makes it possible for us to stand, walk, and run.

Feet have been depicted throughout history by sculptors and painters, often with suggestive beauty. Even as a child Salvatore Ferragamo must have observed this essential part of the body, which he decided to cherish and to study in such depth that it became his vocation in life.

Last October I visited Florence with various intentions in mind: to define the concept of the showing, to visit the museum installed in the magnificent Palazzo Spini Feroni, and to meet its director. I was welcomed splendidly and hit it off immediately with Stefania Ricci, a woman of great sensibility and wide culture, and a worthy director of the museum, who responds with passion and rigor to the principles of Salvatore Ferragamo. She manages a space in which the creation of shoes is emphasized as a work of art, and stands guard faithfully over the spirit of a concept.

Together we toured the several floors of this extraordinary medieval palace, remarkably restored at the present day. What most surprised me was the space where Salvatore himself worked, with 65 other people, on the hand-crafted magic of his creations. The magnificent space in which the *walking dreams* were produced, under his care, had been chosen by Ferragamo himself as the ideal place for the daily performance of his labors. I was delighted by the idea of transforming part of a palace into a shoemaker's workshop. In the place of furniture made of precious woods, paintings by Bernardino Poccetti or Ranieri Del Pace, porcelain, carpets, and silver, there was to be found —as the photographs attest— the spell of a workshop redolent of leather and glue, and cobblers' tools noisily at work producing chimeras fashioned to move.

The Ferragamo family, made up of Mrs. Wanda Miletti, Salvatore's widow, and their six children, possessed the ability and the determination not only to preserve the spirit of the husband and father, but also to expand the Ferragamo firm through other articles of refined creation. This is an idea that the artist had always had in mind, but his devotion and unswerving dedication to the creation of

The White Rose by David Wark Griffith. 1923. The Academy of Motion Picture Arts and Sciences, Los Angeles.

Next page:
Salvatore Ferragamo with Audrey Hepburn in Palazzo Spini Feroni, 1954. Photo Locchi. Locchi Historical Archive, Florence.

"Audrey Hepburn's long, slim foot is in perfect proportion to her height. She is a true artist and a true aristrocat. Audrey is always natural and completely unaffected, whether she is acting or buying shoes or handbags. She can talk intelligently and knowledgeably on philosophy, art, astronomy, and the theatre, and, in my opinion, is the Scandinavian-British aristocratic tradition which began with Greta Garbo and continued with Ingrid Bergman.

Wooden lasts of the famous feet in Palazzo Spini Feroni. Photo David Lees. Time Life, New York.

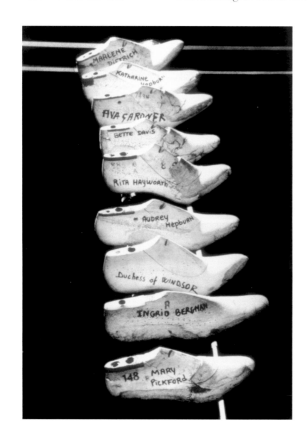

shoes prevented him from carrying it out. It was his descendants who fulfilled this wish of their father. All of them, without exception, work for Ferragamo.

During my brief stay in Florence to work out the details of the exhibition, I was lodged in a charming hotel a few steps from the Ponte Vecchio. I was surprised to find in this sophisticated *albergo*, which belongs to the Ferragamo family but has nothing to do with the world of shoes, the spirit of Salvatore. On entering and leaving the hotel, I would notice on the television screens placed around the hotel the projection of Hollywood classics such as *Sabrina*, in which Audrey Hepburn wears shoes specially created for her by Salvatore Ferragamo, or Walt Disney's *Cinderella*, in which the importance of shoes goes without saying.

I soon learned that the hotel offered free to guests a list of films in which great stars of the silver screen appeared wearing Ferragamo shoes. I gave in to nostalgia and requested a different title every night for the duration of my stay. I relived the unforgettable images that marked an epoch in motion pictures and were decisive in the life of Salvatore Ferragamo. After reaching *The End*, I would look out at the gentle currents of the Arno for a few moments before going to bed.

I was deeply impressed by this will and determination of the children to keep the genius of their father absolutely alive.

I returned to Mexico with the revelation of a story and the discovery of a museum that belongs to the astonishing universe of creation, in which the testimony of a life devoted to the making of shoes combines the perfectionism of a craft and the lively and passionate goal of touching a pair of feet, clothing them, and thus completing the dynamism of a moving sculpture.

While preparing the exhibition, I have often reflected on the talent, conviction, and tenacity of a genuine aesthete who made a real-life movie of his own existence. This mind full of imagination, with a powerful and innate determination, made it possible for the creator to attain the definitive innovation of footwear through constant discoveries and achievements that generated, in accordance with the age, a genuine revolution, recognized the world over.

For Ferragamo, fashion and culture were always linked activities: throughout his career he found inspiration and collaboration with great artists of his time, and commissioned the Futurist painter Lucio Venna to create the advertising for some models of his shoes.

A single curve, the one that outlines a foot in countless variations, was to be the great obsession of his life and the subject of his constant research. There were no limits to experimentation, and on this ambitious –but above all, pleasant– path Ferragamo was able to earn fame by creating vibrant dreams for the feet of aristocrats, princesses, and the most famous actresses of the age.

This exhibition in the Museum of the Palacio de Bellas Artes presents a selection of eighty shoes, shown off by illuminated divas, constituting a brief summary of a career and an obsession.

This enduring passion directed at an object, precise and precious, crafted with the greatest skill, led its creator to definitive success in the most sophisticated world of international fashion. Still more important, however, is the fact that his work has become over time an undeniable and seductive visual language which we are proud to exhibit in this museum.

I am sure it would have been a pleasure for Salvatore Ferragamo to convey, from his Palazzo Spini Feroni to our Palacio de Bellas Artes, an historic showing of his works of art created to touch the feet and beautify them with his ideas, talent, and inventiveness. It is the turn now for the Ferragamo family, and the Salvatore Ferragamo Museum, to share with us their satisfaction at installing in this prestigious Mexican museum, for the first time in Latin America, these magnificent *walking dreams*, and to celebrate them together with us.

Salvatore Ferragamo with the lasts made for his famous customers, 1955. Photo Locchi. Locchi Historical Archive, Florence.

Previous page:
The wooden lasts of feet of members of the diplomatic corps in Palazzo Spini Feroni, 1955. Photo Locchi. Locchi Historical Archive, Florence.

Ferragamo's workshop in Palazzo
Spini Feroni, 1937. Photo Alinari.
Alinari Archive, Florence.

SALVATORE FERRAGAMO, SHOEMAKER AND ARTIST

Stefania Ricci

Salvatore Ferragamo was a creative genius in 20th century footwear. His shoes are works of craftsmanship and art that invite intriguing parallels between lifestyles, architecture, design and art.

Ferragamo liked to call himself a shoemaker, an artisan. His construction techniques, his materials, some also made by hand, such as embroidery work or plaited raffia, and his creation of models have far more in common with a Renaissance *bottega* than a modern fashion atelier. So it's hardly surprising that it was in Florence, cradle of the Renaissance, that Ferragamo decided to open his workshops and company at the end of the 1920s. Like a Renaissance workshop, Ferragamo didn't just design shoes but modelled them as if they were sculptures, directly on wooden lasts reproducing the shape of the feet belonging to his celebrity customers - film stars, nobility, royals. And again, as in the Renaissance, aesthetic development was based on technical expertise and construction know-how and on devotion to craft.

Salvatore, the eleventh of fourteen children, was born in 1898 in Bonito, Southern Italy. His shoemaking vocation emerged very early. At 16, after apprenticeships with the local shoemaker and a luxury shoe shop in Naples, he decided to join his brothers in the United States, thus sharing in the destiny of many Italians who emigrated in pursuit of the American dream to escape poverty and unemployment at home. Ferragamo's main motive, however, was to learn, as he was never content with what he'd already mastered. He realized that in America, where the modern footwear industry had started up only a few years previously, he could further his career in a way impossible in Italy. Having arrived in New York, he moved to Boston and got a job in a factory that made thousands of shoes under the "Queen Quality" label. Salvatore was impressed by the efficiency of American industry but not by the end product. He saw that mass produced shoes were fairly good, with respect to the average in the States, but heavy and ungainly in style and construction when compared to what good shoemakers in Italy could do.

Salvatore persuaded his brothers to move to Santa Barbara on the West Coast, where the nascent film industry was creating potential for makers of luxury hand-made shoes.

Salvatore Ferragamo tests the resilience of his gold sandals, 1956. Photo Locchi, Locchi Historical Archive, Florence.

He opened a small shoe repair and shoemaking shop and in the evenings attended an anatomy course at the local university, driven by his desire to create not only beautiful shoes but ones that were also comfortable and functional.

The opportunity to make a name for himself came from one of his brothers, who worked as a prop man at the American Film Company and managed to get Salvatore his first order, for a batch of cowboy boots. From then on, his shop was besieged by film directors and stars of the silent movie era, such as Pola Negri, Mary Pickford and her sister Lottie, Gloria Swanson and Mae West. When the film industry moved to Hollywood in 1923, Ferragamo followed it and opened a new shop, the Hollywood Boot Shop, in one of the main streets in Beverly Hills, Hollywood Boulevard, on a corner with Las Palmas.

The most famous directors of the period, such as Cecil B. de Mille, James Creuze, David Wark Griffith and Raoul Wash, commissioned Ferragamo shoes for their epic productions (eg. *The Ten Commandments, The Covered Wagon, The White Rose, The Thief of Baghdad).*

To develop his career in the United States, where techniques were already very advanced, and create models without restraints in terms of cost or materials, was a privilege that few Europeans, and no Italians enjoyed at the time. His big problem, however, was to reconcile growing orders with the lack of skilled labour in the handmade shoemaking trade.

In his search for skilled artisans, Salvatore decided in 1927 to return to Italy, choosing Florence as his new base, a city with a concentration of crafts that were becoming increasingly rare and profitable and attracting many foreign buyers, particularly Americans.

Ferragamo, with his intimate knowledge of the American market, its tastes and needs, found Florence the ideal terrain for his inventive spirit. He understood the force of a message that combined a quality, hand-crafted product with the image of such a unique place and that created in the minds of his customers the illusion that to own a pair of Ferragamos was like having a bit of Florence, its art and cultural traditions.

To that fertile terrain Salvatore brought a breath of fresh air, the result of his international experience. In particular, he imported the production processes of the American footwear industry into hand-made shoemaking, thus creating a human assembly line in which each phase was performed by a shoemaker specialized in that part of the job. He introduced the American fitting system, with its more precise numbering not only of foot lengths but also widths, and modified it to his own purposes. He invented new technical solutions, such as the steel shank supporting the arch of the foot, and over the years patented construction techniques that were to change the industry. Ferragamo turned footwear into a research lab where he could study forms, materials and colours. He was particularly interested in experimenting with materials, all materials, from the most valuable and coveted to the newly developed, and even the most traditional, which he transformed in unusual ways and in unexpected colour combinations and decorations. Constantly tuned in to the contemporary world, he was certainly no stranger to what was happening in modern art, architecture and design. From the futurist artist Lucio Venna, he commissioned work for his first advertising campaigns and the logo to print on his footwear label.

Ferragamo creations from the late 1920s and early 1930s were outstanding in the decoration of the uppers and their bold colours, used either alone or in daring combinations in patchworks of fabrics and leathers. The hues of the Southern Italian landscape blend with California's Mexican folklore, the haunting allure of the Giotto and early Renaissance frescoes that grace so many places in Florence, and the colour in motion of the contemporary futurist movement.

While on the one hand Ferragamo studied exclusively ornamental forms that enabled him to finely customize a shoe, he was intensely committed, on the other hand, to making his products functional. Some of his patents changed the history of shoemaking, such as invisible sole stitching systems, methods for cutting uppers from a single piece of leather and decorating leather by abrasion of the top layer only. Of all his inventions though, perhaps the most important was the metal shank, a strong, thin lightweight metal plate reinforcing the arch of the foot and replacing what in traditional Italian shoemaking had been made of leather or a leather by-product.

In the mid '30s Ferragamo switched his main focus of attention to form, which was also the aspect of design that was to be of paramount interest in Italy through the '40s and '50s. Ferragamo shoes in this period were almost works of architecture in their assembly of details, symmetries, in the perfect balancing of weights and dimensions. The cork wedge heel is perhaps the most famous invention from this period, patented in 1937, a good two years before it conquered the world of fashion and became an icon of contemporary taste. And it was developed above all for a functional purpose, to raise the heel and give the arches a stable support. This was also a brilliant solution to a problem that arose at the start of the war in Ethiopia, when the United Nations imposed economic sanctions on Italy, involving, among other imports, the German steel that Ferragamo used to make his shanks. The wedge gave an artist like Ferragamo the chance to deploy his creativity over bigger surfaces than uppers and heels offer. He experimented with many variants on the wedge, both heel and platform, in layers compressed and rounded, sculpted and painted, decorated with fragments of glass mirror or floral-motif brass lattice work sprinkled with stones.

Economic sanctions aggravated Italy's shortage of commodities and energy sources, thus inducing the government to promote the use of local materials, which helped fuel Ferragamo's inventiveness not only on the artistic side but technologically as well. He designed heels made by sewing together wine bottle corks, which he then covered with leather, and patented special processes for making leather substitutes. He invented transparent bakelite heels, articulated wooden soles and soles made of Erinoid or glass. His natural propensity for non-valuable materials, founded on his conviction that luxury resides not in the richness of the materials used but in the underlying concept and the quality of the work, led him in the early '30s to make extended use of hemp and straw based fabrics and woollen thread. He even used cellophane obtained from sweet papers, producing a variety of thicknesses and surfaces – polished or pleated, for example.

Ferragamo thus came to be recognized as a leading exponent of Italy's "autarchic" industry, receiving flattering attention from the Italian press and being widely admired outside the country as well.

Loretta Young in the 40's with Ferragamo's sandals in straw and cork. Salvatore Ferragamo Archive, Florence.

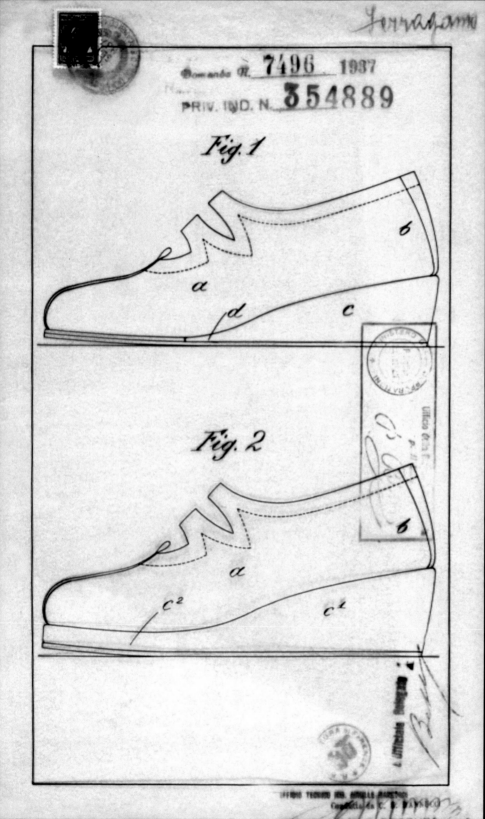

Ferragamo

Domanda N. __7496__ 1937
PRIV. IND. N. 354889

Fig. 1

a *b* *c* *d*

Fig. 2

a *b* *c²* *c¹*

The wedge patent requested
by Ferragamo in 1937.
State Archives, Rome.

"Within weeks, the wedge had
become my popular style. Every
woman who wore it came to me
to extol its comfort. The comfort
was in the cork. Rubber would
have given a jerky, spring step:
cork makes the feet feel as if
they are riding on a cushion.
I patented the design in most
countries of the world. By that
time every shoemaker in the world
was making wedges and to have
sustained my claims I would have
been forced to sue everyone. Their
popularity had spread with such an
extraordinary rapidity throughout
the civilized world that within less
than two years after its invention
86 per cent of all shoes made in
the United States had wedge heels".

Previous page:
In 'Documento Moda' II,
Summer 1942.

Lending ear to his acute business sense, Ferragamo culti-
vated an image of himself as an artisan-artist, getting himself
photographed at a cobbler's bench intent on mounting his lat-
est creation on a wooden last, like a sculptor. Even before the
jet set "rediscovered" Florence in the '50s, Ferragamo was
busy developing relationships with persons of note (royals,
aristocrats, actresses), who flocked to the frescoed Palazzo
Spini Feroni to have their noble feet measured by Salvatore
and learn from the master what was happening in footwear.

The opening of the frontiers after the Second World War
and the resumption of normal trade marked the start of an
extraordinarily fertile period for Ferragamo, and for all Italian
design in fact, which was keen to earn the international criti-
cal acclaim and commercial success it deserved. Salvatore

Salvatore Ferragamo with Major
Mitcheson (representing Norman
Hartnell), Christian Dior and Irene
of Hollywood receiving the Neiman
Marcus Award, the Oscar of
Fashion in 1947. Salvatore
Ferragamo Archive, Florence.

Previous page:
Ferragamo's sandals created for
the Neiman Marcus event, 1947.
Photo Barsotti. Salvatore Ferragamo
Archive, Florence.

Ferragamo became an illustrious exponent of Italian creativity and style in fashion. In
1947, he designed an upper using a continuous thread of thin transparent nylon, thus creating the 'invisible' sandal that won him the Neiman Marcus Prize (the fashion Oscar), in
Dallas, along with Christian Dior. Even though it seems the idea was suggested to him by
an angler on the banks of the Arno who was using transparent line, the invention is still
proof of his capacity to explore everything that comes to hand, from the most traditional
things, such as lace and embroidery (applied however with creative originality), to unexpected materials which thus gain a new lease of life and popularity in footwear. The
invisible sandal caused such resonance in the international press that Salvatore had to
move quickly to register patents, for both the construction of the model, the material it
was made of and the sculpted wedge heel in the shape of an "F" (F for *Ferragamo*) that
supported the sandal.

In this period the study of form was increasingly geared to functionality and extend-
ing fields of use. Heels and soles were thus the prime focus of Ferragamo design throughout the decade, as these two elements determined a shoe's "architecture" and stability.
In 1952, he created a low-cut high-heeled shoe in which the arch was made of the same
leather as the upper, so that the sole proper was limited to the front part and the heel,
the only points of support for the foot. The model was strong but flexible like a glove.
The international press nicknamed it the "gloved arch".

The '50s also saw the design of his shell-shaped sole, which drew inspiration from the
opanke, the North American Indian moccasin, where the idea of the sole becoming the upper
suggested to Ferragamo an elegant, smooth and rounded form. He applied this concept
extensively but the patent achieved fame thanks to a court shoe created for one of the
world's best loved actresses, Audrey Hepburn, who in 1954, fresh from her success in *Roman
Holiday*, went to Florence with Anita Loos to order shoes from the illustrious Ferragamo.

A few years later Ferragamo was working on a metal sole with a highly complex construction aimed at providing the comfort of a leather shoe in spite of the rigidity of metal.
The sole was used in one of the most precious models Ferragamo ever made, an 18 kt gold
sandal for an Australian customer.

Palazzo Spini Feroni, Company headquarters since 1938, was on the list of "places to go" for film stars and other celebs touring Europe. Florence was visited by the Duke and Duchess of Windsor, and the Queen of Denmark, for whom Ferragamo patented a special material, made of the skin of the sea leopard. Princess Soraya chose Ferragamo shoes for her wedding. Hollywood and Cinecittà actresses queued up to order shoes for both on and off the set. Ferragamo created exclusive models for all his customers, as he saw their shoes as extensions of their personalities. He amplified Marilyn Monroe's innate sensuality with her famous 11 cm stiletto-heel pointed shoes (made to exactly the same design for 10 years) that accentuated her hip movement when walking. He worked the same magic with Greta Garbo's austere, almost androgynous beauty and Audrey Hepburn's eternally adolescent charm: two icons, one in lace-ups, the other in court shoes, who perhaps wouldn't have been quite the same without Ferragamo.

Salvatore Ferragamo always analyzed the shape and size of feet, which he believed had much to say about character. In his autobiography, written in 1957 just three years before his death, he put women in three categories, Cinderellas, Venuses and Aristocrats. The Cinderellas, like Mary Pickford, always wear smaller than size 6. They're feminine people, he wrote, who must always have someone loving them to be happy. Venuses wear size 6, like Marilyn Monroe, and are usually beautiful, fascinating and sophisticated. Beneath their exterior though, they love the simple things in life and are doomed to

Following page:
Presentation on Danish television of sea-leopard skin patented by Salvatore Ferragamo in Copenhagen, 1954. Salvatore Ferragamo Archive, Florence.

The Ferragamo boutique on New York's Park Avenue, opened in the 50's. Salvatore Ferragamo Archive, Florence.

be misunderstood. Size 7s and over are worn by Aristocrats, sensitive women who can sometimes be moody. They include Audrey Hepburn and the two great Swedish actresses Greta Garbo and Ingrid Bergman.

In the second half of the '50s, Ferragamo started thinking about the future and how to deal with increasing competition and the demands of international markets.

Italy's economic boom, the appearance of new footwear producers on the international market and growth in domestic demand convinced Salvatore Ferragamo he needed to review his production strategy. In 1948 he had declined an offer from an American producer of $50,000 a year for 20 years to use the "Ferragamo Debs" brand in one of its own lines of industrial shoes. But ten years on he was forced to compromise in order to maintain overall market appreciation of Ferragamo footwear and increase sales. Whilst keeping part of their production artisan in method, Ferragamo designed a number of less expensive lines, using the above mentioned "Ferragamo Debs" and the "Ferrina Shoes" brands, which were made in the UK, 60% by hand and 40% by machine.

At the same time, the Company started to diversify into other products, starting with bags, printed silk scarves (featuring major Italian cities and their art treasures) and, in 1959, a small collection of sportswear for Lord and Taylor, designed by Salvatore's second born Giovanna.

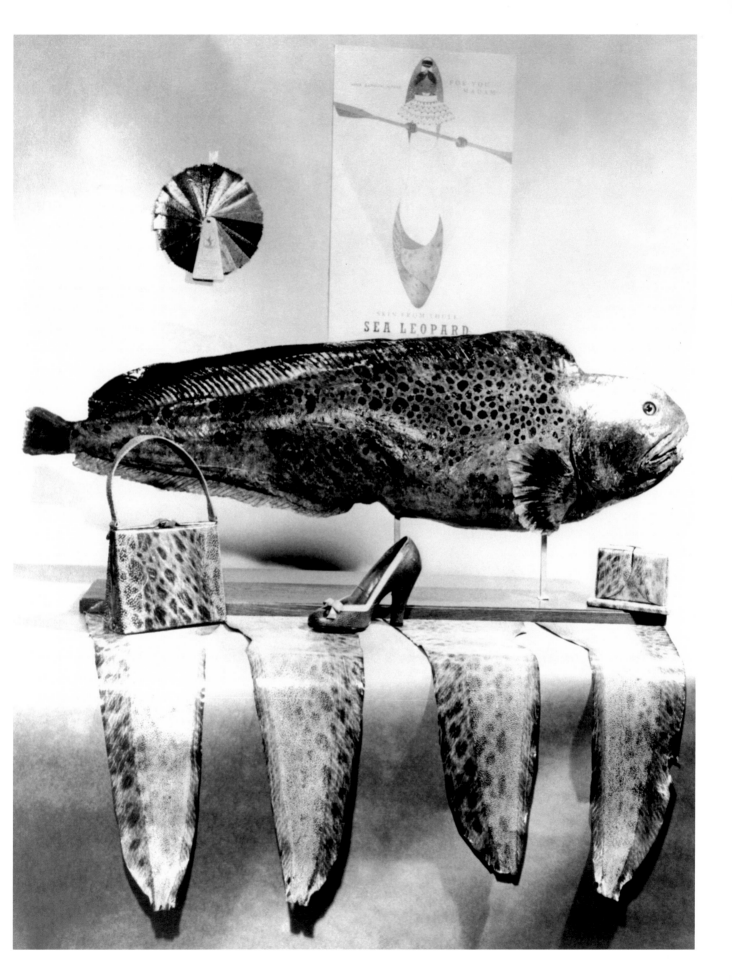

Salvatore died in 1960, leaving his wife and children a company whose name is a synonym for "Made in Italy" and luxury. To history, he left the models and inventions that did so much to shape fashion in the 20th century.

The Ferragamo family: Salvatore Ferragamo with his wife Wanda and their children: Fiamma, Ferruccio, Giovanna, Fulvia, Massimo and Leonardo, 1959. Photo Locchi. Locchi Historical Archive, Florence.

Previous page:
The actress Paulette Goddard in Palazzo Spini Feroni, 1959. Photo Locchi. Locchi Historical Archive, Florence.

Southern
ARGONAUT
Pacific

THE ART OF SALVATORE FERRAGAMO

Margo Glantz

Shoemaking: a lesser trade?

A simple, crafted, hand-made object, like that of ironsmiths, dyers, tanners, the shoe was a useful and necessary addition: there it was in function and in substance. Over the course of the centuries, however, history records numerous exceptions when the artifact was conceived as a specially-designed luxury product: in the twelfth century, queen Eleanor of Aquitaine charged her lover and the arbiter of court fashion, the troubadour Bernard de Bertand, to design sumptuous long gowns with ample trains and buoyant folds, which could not be shown off without their proper complement, a pair of beautiful shoes. Bertand had them made in supple leather with pointed toes. Beautiful but uncomfortable, the feet of the ladies began to ache, a clear sign, it was thought, of both elegance and religious piety.

It has been suggested that the English *court shoe* may have come from this design. Ferragamo designed countless marvelous models of this type of dress shoe, for example, the one fashioned between 1948 and 1950, still in very good condition, with its high Louis XVI heel —slightly curved— and black suede upper perforated on the vamp and quarters with irregular strips of light grey patent leather, and the almost identical but older Fiamma model, also manufactured in Italy between 1928 and 1930, which shows the same irregular strips —a little thicker— in tobacco-colored kid.

If these two models are compared, it is easy to see the similarities and slight differences (the width of the heel and the shape and thickness of the strips of kid), reiterated in the catalogue description that classifies them as art objects, like other kinds of everyday objects: ceramics, glassware. Let us not forget that most museums —among others, the Met in New York, the Victoria and Albert in London, and the Galleria del Costume in the Palazzo Pitti in Florence— reserve a large section of their installations for Fashion Art. As does, since 1995, the Palazzo Spini Feroni, also in Florence, the headquarters of the Ferragamo firm.

Of each of the two models —by no means out of date today—, only one shoe —the left in one case, the right in the other— has been preserved. An announcement I read in an

Salvatore Ferragamo on set in Hollywood. Photo Alinari. Alinari Archive, Florence.

English antique magazine inevitably comes to mind: around 1970 a pair of seventeenth-century shoes turned up, both of them in excellent condition; they were auctioned off at the home of the Lords of Northampton for 20,000 pounds sterling, not because of their perfect condition but because it is so rare to find a complete pair. Nor can I fail to mention here another anecdote that has always astonished me: when Marie Antoinette was guillotined, she let fall her beautiful satin slippers —white?— at the foot of the scaffold. Only one of them was recovered, and displayed by turns in six niches exquisitely lined with light-colored silk during the exhibition organized in Caen to celebrate the second centenary of the French Revolution. Now then, if the niches were lined in white, can it not be deduced that the slipper was of a dark color?

It was in seventeenth-century France that men's shoes made their appearance, adorned with ribbons and equipped with a small heel, called a Louis heel (dubbed a Louis XVI heel in twentieth-century fashion: centuries and titles ride piggyback). In the nineteenth century the ribbons disappeared and, for dancing, men wore fine pumps made of different kinds of leather and graced with a pompom. It is a little-known fact that the name of the Emperor known to history as Caligula —in fact, Gaius Caesar Augustus Germanicus— comes from the Latin word *caliga*, which designated his favorite footwear, a kind of sandal used by Roman legionaries, the soles of which were decorated with gold studs in patterns identifying the particular legion to which the soldier belonged. Roman empresses wore sophisticated sandals with gold soles and strips of precious stones, forerunners of the high-heeled sandals with cleft vamp —of the Manolo Blahnik kind—, distinctive and indispensable signs of high fashion today. I cannot fail to mention a line of footwear invented and patented by Ferragamo during the Second World War, known as the invisible shoe, with an upper made of nylon threads joined down the middle to a vertical strip of leather —red, gold, green, pink, or purple—. The transparent nylon contrasts with the perforated central strip and the dark-colored platform or wedge heel, invented by Ferragamo and designated by the letter "F". Made of cork or wood and lined with leather, it is sometimes the same color as the instep strap and the transversal strip holding together the elegant, superfine threads that leave the foot almost completely exposed. Consider that in the sixteenth century St. Teresa of Ávila (or of Jesus) provoked a schism in the Catholic Church by imposing as a rule the use of austere low-cut sandals to reform the Order of Discalced Carmelites, and that Roman prostitutes decorated the soles of their sandals with the words *follow me*: they left their traces on the sand.

In 1923, at the beginning of his career, Salvatore Ferragamo used sandals to clothe the 12,000 feet of the extras who were to act in Cecil B DeMille's *The Ten Commandments*: elegant women of the time considered it vulgar and even indecent to show their toes and heels. In his autobiography Ferragamo confesses that the first person for whom he made sandals was an Oriental princess he had met when he was living in Santa Barbara —one of the Meccas of the silent movie industry at the time— and who was not in the least averse to displaying her feet. The result: the "Roman" sandal, a variation on the model designed by Ferragamo for the DeMille movie: a flat sandal, graced with a fringe of lace knotted above the ankles and unanimously acclaimed by all the luminaries in the former

solar system of Hollywood. Several year later Ferragamo designed for this woman, of whom we know only that she was a multimillionaire princess, "the rarest and most exquisite shoes of my career", as he recounts in his autobiography. Shoes never seen before, made of hummingbird feathers acquired along the Mexico-California border by one of the many Mexican workers in his employ.

A friend of Hollywood stars, as well as their shoemaker, the Italian Salvatore Ferragamo had been born in 1898 in Bonito, a small village in the vicinity of Naples, "where there was no future for the ambitious", and where the inhabitants had survived for generations by working the land. The eleventh of fourteen children, Ferragamo decided to devote himself to the making of shoes, a trade looked down on by his parents and countrymen:

I had been born to become a shoemaker. I know and have always known it. When I look back… I realize what a constant and unredeemable passion impelled me forward to follow a path sown with difficulties… but I could never leave that predestined path. I would have been struggling against Nature and God. I was born to be a shoemaker…. a profession I did not inherit and whose only explanation can be that in one of my former lives on earth I had been a shoemaker…. How else could this talent I have for design be explained?

On his arrival in Boston in 1914, following in the footsteps of several of his brothers, who like many other Italians had emigrated –and curiously enough all worked in the footwear industry– Ferragamo began to work with his brother-in-law Joseph Covelli at the Queen

Left:
Mary Pickford was the first international star of the silent screen and an important Ferragamo customer. Phototeque, New York.

"… Mary Pickford –Ferragamo remembers– whose feet were the prettiest, the best-shaped and the smallest of all the many film stars I have shod. She is a small woman, of course beautiful, but small; yet her feet, even in proportion to her size, are tiny. The joints inside her feet are like those of a baby, but the toes and the arches are flawlessly shaped. If it were not for their size, I would say that they are the most perfect feet in the world".

Right:
Rudolph Valentino, one of Ferragamo's customers and friends in Hollywood. Experimental Center of Cinematography, Rome.

Quality Shoe Manufacturing Company, at that time one of the most respected footwear manufactures in the United States. Nothing more contrary to his dreams and inclinations:

...They were good shoes by the parameters of machine-made footwear, but not to me, to me they seemed heavy, gross, awkward, not to be compared with those I had seen in Naples, and far, far below the level of excellence I had set myself.... How could I fulfill my task in this labyrinth? I was far from home and I could not be happy there. I was a shoemaker, not a worker destined to carry out a mechanical task: to adjust heels, join pieces of leather, or do the jobs assigned to those who worked in mass production Nothing of the shoemaker's craft was left... 'No, no, I said vehemently [to my brother-in-law], I'm not going to work here, this is not artisan work. I will never have anything to do with machine-made shoes, never!'

Reading his autobiography, one cannot but admire the tenacious stubbornness with which Ferragamo pursued his dream of fashioning shoes as though they were works of art —unique, precious objects, made by hand in accordance with rigorous criteria— and at the same time products intended to improve the health and distinction of those who wore them. In order to do so, as soon as he was able —once he had learned to speak and write English correctly, and had enough money— he studied medicine and chemistry. As a result he was able first of all to gauge the impact of the weight of the body on the feet and thus seek out the best way of making individual lasts, and also to explore the many diverse possibilities that different materials might offer to enhance and renew the art of shoemaking.

I repeat: Ferragamo felt predestined to fulfill a sole task. This is why he decided to leave Boston and follow the rest of his brothers to California, where the motion picture industry was already a powerful force, though still in its beginnings. His first job was for a studio that would later be incorporated into Twentieth Century Fox. He was hired to correct the errors of previous shoemakers, but he soon began to receive special commissions, such as making the boots and shoes for short films and, later on, the footwear used by the characters in one of the most important Hollywood genres, the western.

Perhaps this accumulated experience served him well, for on his return to Europe in 1927 —by which time when he already wore a halo of renown—, having come to the conclusion that there were no craftsmen in the United States and that therefore the only place where it was possible to continue making shoes by hand was Italy. Ferragamo began to produce footwear for

Shoe manufacturing procedure with the upper made out of seamless thread, twine, ribbon and the like, January 28, 1947. State Archives, Rome.

"I took a length of the water–coloured thread and twisted and wound it round the sculptured heel. The result was the 'Invisible' shoe, a style which helped to win for me the Neiman Marcus Award. It was never a good selling line, however, because it leaves the foot so naked and so poised that few women dare accept the extreme challenge to the beauty of their feet".

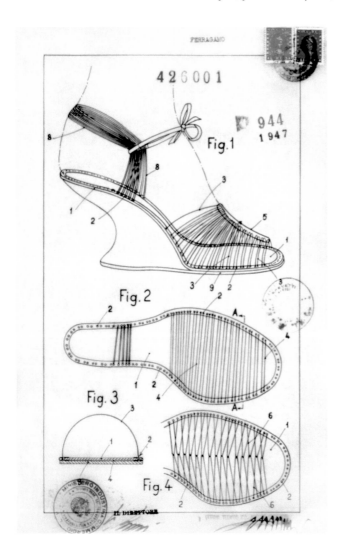

some of the most famous and aristocratic figures of Europe and the entire world. He himself recounted:

My clients included the elite of almost all countries: Queen Elena of Italy, the husband of King Vittorio Emmanuelle III called for me; I made shoes for the wedding of the Princess Marie-José of Belgium, the daughter of the King of the Belgians, with Prince (later, for a short time, King) Umberto; Mussolini came to me with corns and ingrown toenails; his lover, Claretta Pettacci, came as well; Eva Braun, Hitler's lover, arrived surrounded by Nazi bodyguards; one morning four queens were seated at the same time in the four corners of my salon in Rome: the queens of Yugoslavia, Greece, Spain, and of the Belgians. The Maharani of Cooch Behar ordered hundreds of pairs of my shoes. Duchesses and countesses, the wives of the richest businessmen and members of the diplomatic corps, the most famous movie stars, they all came to me, they sent in their orders or bought my shoes where they could find them.

Yes, Ferragamo made shoes for Benito Mussolini: Mussolini, whose defective feet Ferragamo corrected, by means of numerous pairs of high-quality, made-to-measure boots. His lover Claretta adored beautiful shoes and was, according to our shoemaker, totally apolitical, for she was certainly not aware "of the politics her lover controlled. I am convinced she loved him madly, though I am not sure how much he loved her". And he adds, "…when they killed her along with the Duce, there were almost forty pairs of unpaid shoes waiting for her in the Palazzo Feroni" –the beautiful old palace Ferragamo bought in 1938, where he had installed his workshop and which now houses his collection.

With the outbreak of war, Ferragamo faced grave difficulties. Strictly prohibited from using leather, which was reserved exclusively for soldiers' boots, he turned to other kinds of materials, such as those left over from the manufacture of military footwear: felt, hemp, rubber, nylon, cellophane, plastic for the uppers of the shoes, wood and synthetic resins for the heels, and cork for the wedge heels, a prodigious invention which is still seen today on the fashion runway. It is remarkable how Ferragamo's enormous capacity for invention was able not only to compensate for the lack of materials but also to create with new ones many of his most beautiful and perfect models. I will chose one example, which, although it was designed between 1936 and 1938, is a forerunner of those he was to create between 1940 and 1945. It is a sandal with a high (9 centimeters) wooden heel and sling-back, made with woven grass from the Philippines and dyed various colors. The plaited sling-back is adorned with a tassel, the toe is oval-shaped, the

Heel for ladies' shoes, consisting of a metal framework formed by many threadlike elements. Patented January 7, 1956. State Archives, Rome.

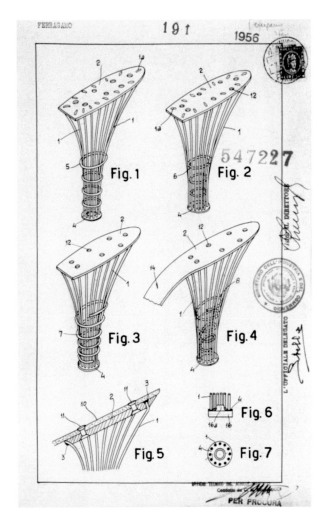

binding is of orange kid, and the lining and sock of beige kid: a truly marvelous, admirable object, worthy of preservation and of being used as a case, a case in which the foot is covered with a weave so fine and fragile and yet so durable, unlike and at the same time similar in its texture to the beautiful carpets of flowers that adorn the forecourts of churches on religious holidays and which are not meant to be stepped on.

Ferragamo also used pointed Oriental toes, turned upwards, for his shoes, and after the war, when skirts began to reach the ankles again and footwear became more stylized, under the influence of Christian Dior, he modified the "F" wedge heels and combined them with different embroidered materials, treated like linen work or lace, similar to a model of gold dress shoes, designed during the war, with lacing in mica tubes. In some of the catalogues and books I have consulted, there appears the photograph of a slender Ferragamo sandal with plaited gold straps forming chains, and a Louis XVI heel —wide at the top, and tapering down to the base without attaining to the stiletto heel so fashionable today— totally encrusted with precious stones. It sold for a thousand dollars in 1956. Most of his shoes, for example the "invisible" sandals, sold for US$27.50 ten years before, the price of four tons of coal. Can this possibly be true?

No obstacle or tragedy was capable of cutting short his inventiveness. He himself made it very clear: "There is no limit to beauty, nor a saturation point for design, and there are endless possibilities to create new and different manufacturing materials".

I wonder if all of his shoes would be comfortable to wear as well as beautiful. Ferragamo insisted they would, and his followers seemed to back him up by returning again and again to order new models, from dress shoes to sporting footwear. Did he not make shoes for Marilyn Monroe, Paulette Goddard, Audrey Hepburn, Pola Negri, Mary Pickford, Valentina Cortese, Lillian Gish, Joan Crawford, Sophia Loren, Greta Garbo,

Gene Tierney, Margaret Lockwood, Barbara La Marr, Vivian Leigh, Bette Davis, Eva Braun, Anna Magnani, Carmen Miranda, Eva Perón, Dolores del Río, Jean Harlow, Alicia Markova, Ava Gardner, Hedy Lamarr, Susan Hayward, Claire Booth Luce, the Duchess of Windsor…?

There are many photographs showing how Ferragamo worked, alongside his collaborators installed in the spacious, high-ceilinged rooms of the Palazzo Feroni, with its stucco decorations over the arches and Salvatore moving between the work tables overseeing his footwear. We can admire the hundreds of lasts hanging like still lifes from special stands, all meticulously classified in accordance with the category of the users: the diplomatic corps, the ruling families, European aristocrats, movie stars… Finally, several photographs show him bent over the feet of a celebrity, gauging with his delicate, sensitive hands their firmness, beauty, or defects.

The shoes of Salvatore Ferragamo, this man of humble origins, were fashioned with skill, rigor, and affection, like the shoes Juan José Arreola describes in his story "Letter to a Shoemaker", published in the book *Varia invención*. In it he reproaches a cobbler for the terrible job he did of mending a pair of exceptional shoes:

Those I gave you to mend were admirable shoes that had served me faithfully for many months. My feet took to them like a fish to water. More than shoes, they seemed to me a part of my own body, a kind of protective wrapping that gave firmness and confidence to my step. Their leather was really my own skin, healthy and resistant. Except that they were showing signs of wear…. I should inform you that I am utterly ignorant in matters of footwear. All I know is that there are shoes that have made me suffer and others, on the contrary, that I remember with tenderness, so soft and flexible they were.

Left:
Salvatore Ferragamo with Gene Tierney, 1951. Photo Locchi. Locchi Historical Archive, Florence.

Right:
Salvatore Ferragamo with Sophia Loren, as she tries on a sandal of Tavarnelle lace, 1955. Photo Meldolesi, Rome. She launched the new Ferragamo invention, the sea-leopard skin, at the Club Open Gate in Rome.

Ferragamo was convinced that, well shod, no foot could suffer; on the contrary, properly shod, feet should never be stricken with the ailments common to them through the ages: bunions, corns, torn or ingrown toenails. For him, these defects were corrected by proper footwear. For a long time a problem troubled him: how best to measure the feet in order to construct the perfect last and the kind of shoe that would serve as a second skin. Like the Arreola character who scolds the cobbler for his incompetence, Ferragamo blamed bad shoemakers for ruining their customers' feet. "In fact –he explains–, a well shod foot never grows old... My most recent confirmation of this is the feet of Gloria Swanson, who visited me a little while ago in my Florence salon. When I took her feet in my hands I found them as young and beautiful as the first time I made shoes for them, more than thirty years before". Gradually, in the course twenty years of observation, and based on the knowledge of medicine and chemistry he had patiently acquired, the secret was revealed to him. Like Newton when he discovered the law of gravity, Ferragamo found that the entire weight of a standing body is distributed over the arches of the feet, that only a tiny area (around seven centimeters) sustains us, and, when we walk, the weight of our bodies swings from one foot to another. Before proceeding to build the perfect last, it is necessary to take measurements, from the back to the lower extremities, in order to ascertain the particular characteristics of each person: the width, length, and height of the instep, the size and shape of the toes and heel, and above all the type of arch. Throughout his career, Ferragamo invented and patented various ways of making shoes lighter, as when, during the metal shortage of the war years, he covered the arch with kid rather than with the leather used for the sole, replacing the thin metal arch that had previously been employed.

I will end this text with the words he himself used to describe his passion:

I love feet. They speak to me. When I take them in my hands I feel their strength, their vitality, or their defects. A good foot of firm muscles and a fine arch is a delight to touch, a masterpiece of divine craft. A bad foot, with its toes twisted, its joints defective, its ligaments loose under the skin, is an agony. When I take those feet in my hands, I am consumed by anger and compassion, anger that I cannot make shoes for all of humanity and compassion for those who must walk in pain.

C- 178

THE VOICE OF YOUR SHOES

Alberto Ruy Sánchez

It was when I began to work as editor of the erotic magazine *El Jardín Perfumado* –a kind of *Playboy* with fewer blonds and more erotic customs of far-off peoples– that women's shoes entered my life, without my suspecting or wishing it, and did away with my peace of mind.

For the first time, the principal cause of this tumult was not so much the ostentatious eroticism of the magazine, which has always meddled in my relations with other people, exercising its imaginative power over what I do and what I am, as the long, dark, stone corridor I used to walk down to get to my office.

It all began with a certain gentle melancholy, like a restless dripping before the steps of someone who reminded me of a woman: the one who left me to the sound of high heels calmly tapping out her abandonment down that long, marble corridor.

Many years have passed and I still hear her walking away when the silence thickens toward nightfall. I have forgotten her telephone number, the date of her birthday, many of her words, and even the exact shade of her eyes. But not her shoes. Never the voice of her shoes.

Because, when I least expect it, that insistent voice issues from another pair of heels and all but calls out my name with their tapping. A sort of monotonous Morse code of farewell fading away down the stairs. It took me a long time to stop feeling sad at the music of a pair of high heels vanishing into the distance. But like so many things in life, the period of mourning came to an end, and shoes stopped leaving traces of my amorous abandonment. Then my problems with them increased, and that somber dripping turned into a turbulent stampede of soles that invaded even my dreams.

I cannot recall who decided we should rent an office in one of those tall, old buildings downtown, at the end of a corridor along which people could be heard from the moment they stepped out of the elevator. I wonder how many of them realized they were entering an echo chamber. No one, perhaps, except those of us who worked amidst that sporadic ambulant music.

When I would get out of the elevator, suddenly assailed by an amplified awareness of my footsteps, I used to feel like taking off my shoes and walking on tiptoe. Or, if no one

Dolores Del Río, one of Hollywood cinema's most famous bathing beauties and a Ferragamo customers. Corbis/Grazia Neri Archive, Milan.

was with me, of doing just the opposite and tap-dancing my way down the hallway, in a pale imitation of Gene Kelly in *Singing in the Rain*. The first time I did so I was wearing new shoes that had gotten a little wet in the street.

When I took my first tentative but obstinate tango lessons, the deserted shadows of the corridor were ideal for practicing the long steps and linked turns, and for listening to the continual squeaking of my shoes as they dragged across the floor, which my teacher told me ought to be heard in the background of a well-danced tango.

My teacher Paulina, who was a psychoanalyst from Buenos Aires as well as a dancer, claimed that, thanks to the tango, she had learned to read the complicated family histories of people in their shoes. She used to say of her patients: "I lay them down on the analyst's couch not so much so that they can relax and talk without looking at me, as in order to be able to look their shoes up and down. When I actually reach the point of helping them with their problems, I make them dance the tango until it begins to affect their shoes. Because everything you are and love is in your shoes: family dramas, tension, energy." How I miss my tango teacher! And her shoes, so high and yet so free, which would suddenly cleave the air between my legs and then tilt her toward me perfectly when we went through certain steps in which her balance depended on my shoulders or my hands.

During those long solitary hours in my office, separated from the corridor by no more than a wooden door and some smoked glass, I learned thanks to Paulina's obsessions to recognize people by their gaits, agile or dragging, brusque or light. Dawdling collection agents or others in a hurry, leisurely or anxious visitors forecast the essential features of their faces through their footwear. All of them brought the pitter-patter of their shoes into the building.

The models who posed for the magazine were the easiest to identify. I learned to gauge a woman's measurements by the way she approached me without knowing I was listening. Balance has its own music. And every step betrays the excesses of a body fore and aft. The harmony of those who feel at home in their skins is a composition of steps so exceptional that it cannot be concealed. The deepest and most contradictory clues to a personality are revealed by walking. It was almost possible to tell by a model's steps, before seeing her, whether or not she was going to be interesting photographed in the nude. The inner angel or demon takes controls first of all of a person's shoes.

Finally what I feared came to pass. As a result of this concentrated attention on the world of women's footwear, there came the day when I fell hopelessly in love with a woman because of the unexpected squeaking of her shoe soles.

From the moment she walked out of the elevator she conveyed such a strangely perfect harmony in her first three steps that I was violently distracted from the proofs I was correcting. On hearing the elevator doors close behind her I was invaded by a disquieting sensation of intimacy. She was far away and yet near, all too near. The voice of her shoes was whispering in my ear.

She was not yet halfway down the corridor when her steps began to grow longer, one of them producing something like a muffled groan, and suddenly there followed a sort of amorous whimper. A squeak from her shoe that at once conveyed to me the sensation of her entire body. I felt a rush of blood to my toes, my hands, and, of course, my sex.

In 'Novus', Spring/Summer 1940.

Page 46:
The actress Ida Lupino in the 40's. Corbis/Grazie Neri Archive, Milan.

Page 47:
Katherine Hepburn in George Cukor's *The Philadelphia Story*, 1940. Her unconventional looks made their mark at a time when the screen was dominated by more glamorous beauties. Corbis/Grazie Neri Archive, Milan.

Salvatore Ferragamo showing one of his younger employees how to make a shoe. Salvatore Ferragamo Archive, Florence.

There are people who blush in such situations; I tingle awkwardly at my extremities. And by a strange association of images and ideas I had the intuition –nor was I mistaken, as I later confirmed– that the amorous shoes approaching me resembled the steep high heels that Marilyn Monroe was wearing in the scene where the gust of air from the subway vent lifts up her skirt. And I also saw that these ones were very red, the color of blood in ferment.

Needless to say, this clear, striking, and precise vision robbed me of my tranquility for several years. But what followed was more terrible still, and continues to reverberate noisily in my life.

The second half of the corridor seemed to last an eternity. I considered getting up and running toward this woman I had never seen and whom nevertheless I felt I knew intimately. Whom I knew at once in that facet that is revealed exclusively by shoes. It is a mistake to think that it is only by long hours of conversation that one person can get to know another. There are couples who become thoroughly acquainted by dancing, without ever exchanging a word. And those who by making love know more about someone than if they had read his memoirs or listened to a recording of his appointments with his analyst. In the same way there is a dimension of people that emerges, and with luck even blooms, through their shoes. I call to mind at once the sort of crumpled sunflower, full and large and aggressive, that Catherine Zeta-Jones wears on her sandals, and which has always seemed to me the other side of her lips and her limpid and docile beauty.

But I did not get up to meet her. I controlled myself in order not to frighten her with my impatient breathing or the obsessive look in my eyes, and I waited for her. Every three or four steps, another squeak. I suffered through and longed for each one of them.

I knew exactly how many steps were required to get to my door. But I knew it almost musically, as a rhythmic scale rather than an abstract number. Just as one can know a telephone number by the little melody of ten notes it makes on the keyboard when dialed rather than by the numbers that form it. And I began to feel a sense of urgency as the little song of her steps toward my door failed to complete itself. I even felt suddenly afraid. What if she is here by mistake and realizes she is on the wrong floor before she reaches my door? Again I had the urge to open before she knocked but again I held back. It is always a mistake to throw oneself at a woman, whoever she may be. Impossible as it was not to feel and to dream of her avalanche.

When her feet came to a halt, brushing the skin of her heels, and her knuckles knocked on the glass pane of my door, she gave me another obvious clue to the inner music of her soul. When I saw her smile, I was her prisoner.

I tried to keep my eyes from examining her shoes too insistently. That can sometimes be as coarse and indiscreet as peeking down a woman's cleavage to admire a line of lingerie that peeps out like a bridge spanning two tempting hills. Better to contain oneself, although the gaze leads one instinctively to seek, behind and through the lace, the depths of that brief abyss which, to be sure, is more guessed at than seen. The same with shoes. To stare at them can be felt by some women as an invasion of their intimacy. And of course they want us and do not want us to look. What Madonna invented by wearing her lingerie over other pieces of clothing is what a woman's shoes almost always do: they are intimate wear that often show itself off with false innocence. In fact they exhibit themselves with theatrical pride. In the case of shoes, all modesty, timidity, or discretion is play acting. A woman's shoe is always an intimacy that shows its face in public.

It is the same with the mouth, which, as I have tried to explain on other occasions, is the most malleable and sensitive sexual organ we possess. And we carry it on the outside, smearing it happily or with routine indifference against the faces of many of the people we meet everyday. A woman's shoes are the most daring, the most indiscreet and expensive, the most hand-crafted and socially shared lingerie possessed by human beings. A showy or discreet shoe does not conceal the obscenity of the foot but rather reveals in code a woman's ability to smile with deep, perverse gaiety. One need only contemplate that marvelous scene that life so often offers us: a woman trying on shoes in front of a mirror. She stands up and examines them from above, joining them together. Then she twists her neck back to see how they look from behind. She lifts one foot and examines it again. She sits down and crosses her legs in order to move the tip of one shoe gently back and forth. And then a broad smile lights up her face, without even looking at the mirror. Not a laugh to be shared with those present but a smile: the sign that she has been inwardly moved. Her most intimate being is gladdened by a desire we shall never know with certainty or precision.

That is why it had to be precisely Madonna who one day showed us on screen, in the

Salvatore Ferragamo with the actress Anna Magnani in Palazzo Spini Feroni as she tries on one of the 1955 models. Photo Locchi. Locchi Historical Archive, Florence.

mid-1990s, a pair of Ferragamo stiletto-heeled shoes, entirely of black lace above, with the top of the heel open, the instep bulging under her lingerie as she walked, and the toes partly hiding and partly revealing her flaming red toenails from behind a dark latticework which at that moment hardly deserved to be called simply a shoe. It is very likely, in fact, that Madonna was inspired by a similar pair of shoes by the same designer that Anna Magnani had worn forty years before. And the film in which Madonna displays them is set precisely in those far-off years of the twentieth century: *Evita*. I have seen it more than twenty times just to admire in movement the wide range of footwear she uses. I know by heart the moments when a full-length take will allow me that instant of bliss, that brief glimpse into her deepest intimacy. I would guess that more than twenty pairs of shoes appear on screen, each one different but with a similar personality. Aspects of a Madonna indomitable even to herself that go beyond disguise, beyond the character she embodies for the producers, beyond the representation fashioned by another. There is a pair of shoes made entirely of brightly-colored laces –reds, greens, and blues–, like streamers or the tangled strings of a bathing suit about to fall. There are others of modest little black bows which a single glance shows will not long remain untied. And there are many that seem to be made of supple animal hides, such as soft suede in an ardent and heightened chestnut tone: mature fire. Those with gilded and silvered laces are the most common: they show a superficial aspect of Madonna that is at times not so very different from what others wear. As if she were saying: I too am like you. But it is not long before she puts on something exceptional again, displaying ostentatiously another active aspect of her rigorous and intimate originality.

The shoes of an actress inevitably form a part of her soul that she can neither conceal nor disguise. Her shoes can even become an emblem of her biography. One has only to consider the low, discreet sandals of Ingrid Bergman. The same ones regardless of the role she was playing. As if she always wore the same shoes. They reveal her need to descend, to appear less tall, but also her freedom from an artificial, recherché glamour. They show an insecurity with respect to her height and a confidence in her natural and portentous angelic beauty. And the primary advantage for her of maintaining bodily comfort without sacrificing the impeccable –which is to say, the angelic– beauty of the sandals. Fullness without coquetry. Her successive love affairs with Petter Lindstrom, Roberto Rosellini, Robert Capa, and Lars Schmidt can almost be understood thus: in each one she sought out the beauty of a romance as like as two beautiful sandals. As she recounts with great naturalness in *My Story*. Although the moralists of the United States Senate gravely condemned her as a demon of perversion when she fell in love with Rosellini, she simply says she was the same woman. With sincerity she states that she had "gone from saint to whore and back to saint again." But she underlines: "and all in one and the same life".

Beyond the social condemnation, shoes included, it hurt her to realize what a confused illusion lovers and shoes create in one: in the end no one can really fill four shoes at the same time. The Ferragamo shoes of Ingrid Bergman, with their display of exaggerated simplicity that so contrasts with the rest of his designs, demonstrate that a taut and complex thread is drawn between shoes and the varying desires they provoke in women, making the desire for monogamy and the desire for polygamy one and the same well- or ill-tied lace around the ankles of all women: like two wings of the same bird or a single pair of shoes.

The shoes of Marilyn Monroe have always made me think of that false innocence of hers, which contained something of truth but was overwhelmed by her exuberant sensuality. Her simple but sensual shoes evoke sensuous feet and a swaying body. Their pointed toes and slight forward slant from very high heels recall her in some of her most frequently photographed gestures, offering herself and at the same time denying herself from the curved balcony of her body. With shoes so predisposed, so near to the physical and emotional trampoline, there goes the risk of a fatal fall. And her famous "stiletto" heels were a kind of weapon that frightened and attracted men, but which sooner or later

Marilyn Monroe, a sex symbol of the century, was one of Ferragamo's most famous customers. Her shoes, signed by Ferragamo, were bought at an auction at Christie's in New York in October 1999 and now they are part of the Museum collection. 1962. Photo Allan Grant. Time Life, New York.

Ingrid Bergman and George Sanders in Roberto Rossellini's 1953 film *Viaggio in Italia*. All of Bergman's shoes were made by Ferragamo. AFE, Historical Archive of Cinema, Rome.

she would turn against herself. Shoes are biography, no doubt about it.

I was turning all of this over in my mind while I tried not to stare at the red shoes of the woman who knocked on my door that summer. I asked her to sit down in one of the uncomfortable wooden chairs I had in my austere office and I sat in front of her on the same side of the desk. She introduced herself. Her name was Raquel. She was a writer and was interested in offering me a highly original project for the magazine. To take a series of erotic photographs in which the women and some of the men wore only shoes. But with a major challenge for the photographer and the graphic designers: to make the footwear add a daring touch to the nudity, an erotic revelation clearly more intense than if the shoes had not been there. She would direct the shoot and would write a brief text for each man and woman in which the combination of shoes and nudity was rendered intriguing and suggestive.

Raquel was an exceptional woman, a Mediterranean beauty of keen intelligence. With great firmness in her words and in her body. Capable of being interested with equal intensity —and a complete lack of superficiality— in fashion and in poetry. And as she explained her project to me and showed me a couple of nude images of herself as an example of what the piece might be like, she put her feet before me and looked me in the eyes, virtually challenging me to concentrate on her face and not be drawn down by the naked curve of her foot slipped into a snakeskin shoe swinging gently toward me. She was offering me a bite, I thought: her foot is like a pale apple. A piece of fruit, half-eaten and, at the same time, offered up between the jaws of her shoe.

We did the piece. Nine women wearing the shoes of their choice shown in images unusual for their perspectives and their insouciance. The little biographies of each pair of shoes written by Raquel said more about their subjects than any other type of portrayal could have. I asked her to be one of the models, the last one. The photographs she had shown me were my principal argument. And however much she said she did not want to do it, she had already done it after all and just wanted to be convinced. The shoes she was wearing during our interview had something that struck me immediately. A sort of earring that hung from the lace wrapped around her ankle. When I finally dared to look closely at her feet I asked her about that little piece of silver on each shoe. She raised her hand to her head and drew back the hair covering her ears, revealing a pair of earrings identical to the filigree of her shoes.

"What a good idea, I said, matching earrings and shoes. I don't think anyone has ever done it before." She stared at me strangely and said very slowly: "Don't you see? Not only do they match. They also hook together perfectly. And when they hook together they produce a little jingling, like tiny silver bells that can only be heard close to the ear.

To yours and mine". My jaw dropped, as I drew the obvious conclusion: that her ankles and her ears could only come together in that amorous position which would raise her legs so high they would frame her lovely face between those disquieting red shoes. I imagined so many things as she smiled at me. As I approached my face to her mouth. A jingling only she and I could hear. And I fully understood, at that moment, from what amorous universe and from what keen carnal imagination came the squeaking that has since possessed me. The deepest voice of her shoes.

Lucio Venna, advertising design for Ferragamo, 1930. Museo Salvatore Ferragamo, Florence.

I discovered that the weight of the body, when standing, drops vertically on the arches of the feet, as the plum-line shows.

SALVATORE FERRAGAMO

CATALOGUE OF WORKS

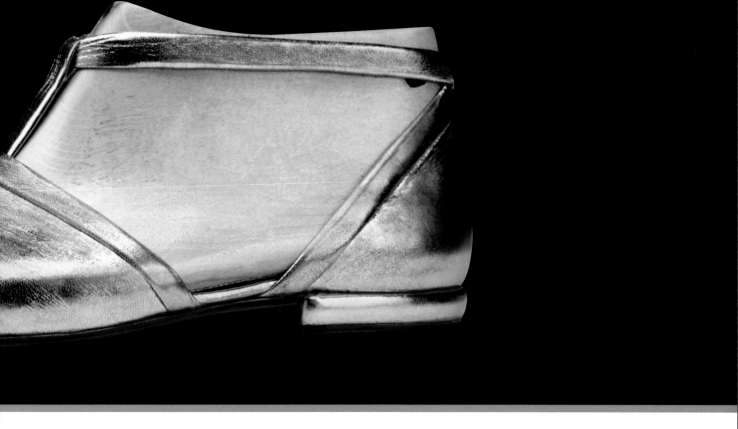

1 Copy, 1985

Length: 26 cm; heel: 1.5 cm

Upper made in two pieces of gold kid with Oriental pointed and turned up toe. Instep strap joined to strap at vamp center. Low heel covered in kid. Leather sole.

This model is copied from the one created by Salvatore Farragamo in Hollywood in 1924 for the film *The Thief of Baghdad* directed by Raoul Walsh and starring Douglas Fairbanks senior.

2 Court shoe, 1927

Length: 21 cm; heel: 7.5 cm
Label: Ferragamo's Creations. Florence Italy
Factory stamp: Made in Italy
Series number, last, and size: 05 05/4

Dark grey kid upper with geometrical decoration in pearl-grey silk chain stitch. Square-cut vamp and back. Binding in hand-stitched black silk thread. Round toe. Curved Louis XV heel in wood covered with grey kid. Beige kid lining and sock. Leather sole.

This shoe was created by Salvatore Ferragamo just after his return to Italy from the United States. The Louis XV heel was fashionable at that time, and this type of sole, extremely narrow under the arch, was often used in his early models. The classic style of the shoe is modified by the slightly squared vamp, and is updated with a refined geometric pattern embroidered on the upper with a labyrinth motif. Ferragamo's design was influenced by avant-garde artistic tendencies of the period, including Futurism and Cubism. The geometrical designs on this shoe can be compared to the fabric designs of Sonia Delaunay.

3 Laced shoe, 1930

Length: 22 cm; heel: 8 cm
Label: Ferragamo's Creations. Florence Italy
Factory stamp: Hand Made in Italy
Series number, last, and size: E 20005 0368 4 1/2 B

Six sets of eyelets. Upper and tongue in beige-tinted fish skin. Brown silk-cord lacing with fish-skin tassels. Round toe. High heel in wood with curved front surface. Beige kid lining and sock. Leather sole.

The oxford, the comfortable walking shoe derived from the shoes worn by English men, was called the *Francesina* in Italy. It was a popular style for everyday wear, with either a high heel in leather or a low Cuban heel and an upper in lizard, crocodile, or fish skin. In the November 1932 issue of the Italian women's fashion magazine 'La Donna', an article stated: "The modern Cinderella exacts contributions for her shoes from the entire planet. From the ruminants to the sharks, from the alligators to the snakes, from the meek goat to the harmless toad, the frog and the lizard of Java. All Noah's ark has been called upon to provide a contribution for the shoes of the modern woman." The use of the skins of local fish in footwear was encouraged by the Fascist regime's restrictive policies, which forced the use of autarkic products. Within a few years these restrictions led to Ferragamo's development of designs employing wedge heels in cork and wood and uppers in raffia and plastic. Ferragamo's experimentation with new materials dates from the beginning of his career in the United States, when he fashioned a shoe upper from hummingbird feathers.

4 Laced shoe, 1928-1930

Length: 22 cm; heel: 9 cm
Label: Ferragamo's Creations. Florence Italy
Factory stamp: Hand Made in Italy

One set of eyelets. Brown suede upper perforated by two strips of natural kangaroo skin from waist to eyelets. Point at back seam. Oval toe. High heel in wood covered with brown suede. Beige kid lining and sock.

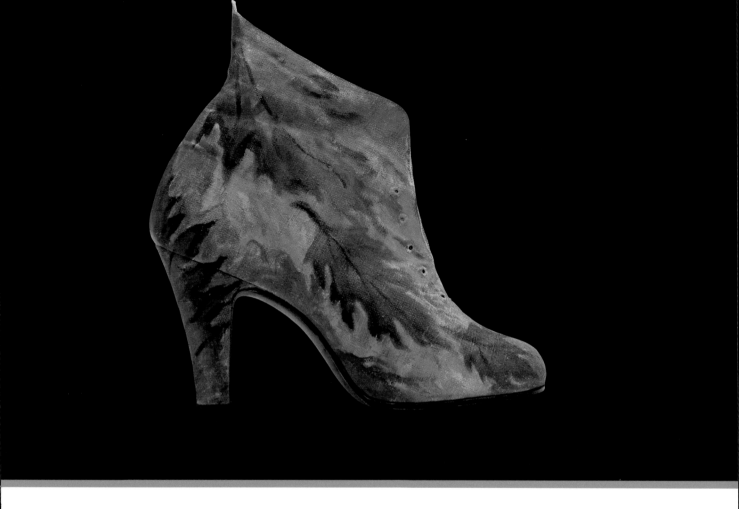

5 Laced boot, 1930

Series number, last, and size: 0S 178/1 5 B 510

Three set of eyelets. Canvas upper hand-painted with leaves in tones of brown. Point at back seam. Round toe. High heel in wood covered with hand painted canvas. Beige kid lining and sock. Leather sole.

This shoe was designed and painted for a specific client and never produced in series.

6 Pull-over, 1930

Length: 23 cm; heel 6 cm

Prototype sandal. Gold kid upper. Three strips of gold kid in decreasing sizes form a pyramid shape on the vamp top. Ankle strap. Square toe. High heel in layers of brass in decreasing sizes repeats the pyramid motif.

In the twenties and thirties, the sandal came back into fashion. The open shoe had been abandoned in the Victorian period, when it was considered unseemly for women to expose their feet. During the twenties, sandals were designed with a closed toe and heel and were open at the sides with crossed lacing. Not until 1930 was the term adopted to identify footwear destined not only for the beach but also for daytime wear, with the toe and/or the heel open and a strap around the ankle. In his autobiography, Ferragamo recounted that his first sandals were created in Hollywood for the film *The Ten Commandments*. He consulted the local library with the hope of finding documentation on Egyptian designs, but only found material on one type of sandal with a low heel and a single lacing. Finding no adequate resources, his first sandal design involved a good deal of imagination. Oriental, Egyptian, classical, and fin-de-siècle themes dominated fashion in the thirties, and Salvatore Ferragamo's footwear designs closely reflected these trends. Even though the materials were sometimes unusual and the design fantastic, the shoes always respected the fundamental rules concerning the support and comfort of the foot.

7 Laced shoe, 1935-1938

Length: 21.5 cm; heel: 10 cm
Label: Ferragamo's Creations. Florence Italy
Factory stamp: Made in Italy
Series number, last, and size: FA 900 04

Five sets of eyelets. Black antelope upper with padded collar and snap clo-
sure. Black antelope tongue. Black silk-cord lacing with black antelope tassels. Prow toe. High heel in wood covered with black antelope. Beige kid lining and sock. Leather sole.

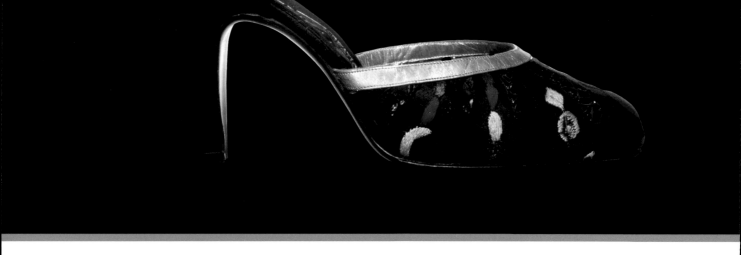

8 Black satin shoe, 1930-1935

Length: 23.5 cm; heel: 8 cm
Label: Ferragamo's Creations. Florence Italy
Factory stamp: Hand Made in Italy

Vamp formed of black satin bands, embroidered with satin-stitched geometrical designs in multicolored silk threads, joined together by bands of black Tavarnelle needlepoint lace. Vamp edged in silver kid. Scalloped, black satin quarters. Silver kid ankle strap with metal buckle. Pointed toe. High heel in wood covered with satin. Black satin soak. Leather sole.

Local cottage industry was entrusted with the embroidery of the uppers. The type of lace used for the upper of this shoe is called Tavarnelle needlepoint lace and was produced at the Convent of San Donato in Poggio and at the lace centers of Passignano, Mercatale, Greve, and Tavarnelle. The lace produced in Tuscany was similar to Venetian needlepoint lace, although less refined. It was primarily used for articles of intimate clothing, yet its robust texture allowed Ferragamo to use it for the uppers of his shoes. Volutes, leaves, flowers, medals and fans on a net or squared ground, often with the addition of embroidery or appliqué, were also the motifs most favored by Ferragamo, who chose to exploit the distinct local style to promote his shoes and to demonstrate the importance of high quality work, done entirely by hand, in a world increasingly threatened by machine production.

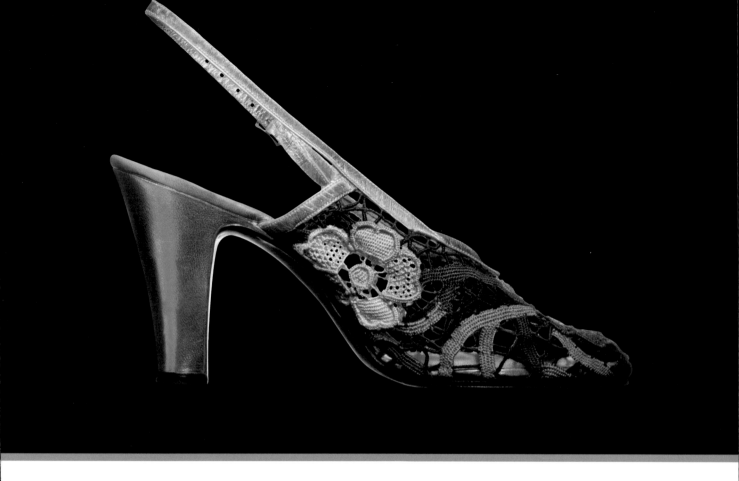

9 'Follia' sandal, 1935

Length: 22 cm; heel: 8 cm
Label: Ferragamo's Creations. Florence Italy
Factory stamp: Hand Made in Italy
Series number, last, and size: OS 221/2 510 4B

Closed toe. Upper in black Tavarnelle needlepoint lace with multicolored floral
decoration. V-shaped vamp edged with gold kid. Sling-back with metal buckle.
Oval toe. High heel in wood and insole edge both covered with gold kid. Beige
kid sock. Leather sole.

10 Pull-over, 1930

Length: 23 cm; heel: 7.5 cm

Model for laced shoe in black suede with appliqué squares in green, yellow, pink, and blue suede outlined in white silk scallop stitch. Black silk cord lacing. Slightly pointed toe.

Salvatore Ferragamo's revolutionary attitude to shoe-making must been seen against the cultural environment which had developed in Europe before the 1930s, as it helps explain the widespread acceptance of his work. The shoe became not only the perfect piece of high quality artisan's work but also the field for independent research into form, material and color, with choices made in a collective climate of experimentation, in the broader context of twentieth-century artistic enquiry.

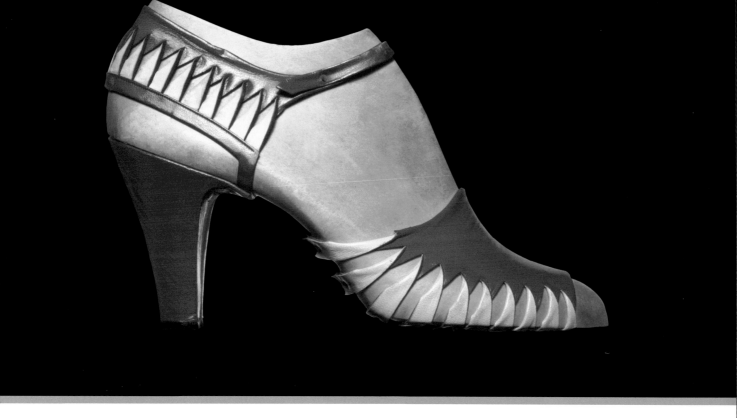

11 Pull-over,1935

Length: 23.5 cm; heel: 7.5 cm

Prototype sandal. Upper formed of a wide red kid band cut at the edges to form strips, which are twisted to expose white kid lining. Sling-back repeats motif of upper. Red kid instead strap. High heel covered with red kid.

Ferragamo's creative search for formal and technical innovations was affirmed in the complex structure of this prototype.

12 Sandal, 1930-1935

Length: 22.5 cm; heel: 4 cm
Label: All hand made. Pompeian Shoes. Florence Italy
Factory stamp: All hand made
Series number, last, and size: E 4042 4B

Upper embroidered in petit point in polychrome cotton thread in a geometrical design to create a patchwork effect. Closed toe. Lateral vamp decoration in blue kid forming two 'wings'. Blue kid tubular strips sewn around insole continues to form sling-back with button-hole and spherical button. Round toe. Round heel in cork. Beige kid sock and lining with blue kid heel sock. Leather sole.

The trade mark Pompeian shoes, which appears on the label of these sandals, refers to a series of designs destined for export, which were produced over a long period of time by Ferragamo. The name was inspired by the archaeological discoveries made at Pompeii in 1927.

13 Sandal, 1937

Length: 22 cm; heel: 3 cm
Label: Ferragamo's Creations. Florence Italy
Factory stamp: Hand Made in Italy
Series number, last, and size: NZ 221 4 1/2 B/3

Upper composed of natural raffia with crocheted floral decoration in orange, blue, green and red. Sling back in woven natural raffia. Laced at ankle in plaited raffia with metal tassels. Insole edge cover in natural hemp. Heel made of corks. Natural kid sock. Leather sole.

Salvatore Ferragamo's return to Italy in 1927 from America saw the emergence of a defined style, based on an original combination of luxury materials with more unusual ones, which remained essential ingredients in his works over the decades. His particular sensitivity in the use of materials was first evident in his work with luxury skins with their varied surfaces, creating surprising results through skillful color and texture combination. The use of patchwork with calf alternating with squares of crocodile and suede or of different colored suedes geometrically arranged are the most obvious examples of how he revised the treatment of more traditional skin. It was a natural progression from the experimentation with established materials to the introduction of more unusual ones. In 1930 he began using fish skins dyed in a variety of colors, embroidered cotton, lace, black and colored grosgrain, woven bark, cylindrical corks, sewn and covered in kid, and moved onto the use of hemps, raffia, grass from the Philippines, and modern cellophane. The most successful materials used for footwear were straw and raffia. They were employed in shoes that were destined not only for beach wear, but for formal and city models. The materials were popular because of their low cost and light weight. These materials had been used by Florentine milliners and accessories craftsmen since the eighteenth century, but Ferragamo was one of the first Italians to use them in the design of shoes.

14 Pull-over, 1935-1936

Length: 23.5 cm; heel: 9 cm

Prototype court shoe. Gold kid upper with painted circular decoration in white, bordered with chain stitch in black silk thread. V-shaped vamp. Round toe. High heel covered with gold kid.

This model closely resembles the Sparta model, depicted in the sketches for a publicity brochure designed by Lucio Venna for Ferragamo in 1930. The similarity between the shoes in Venna's brochure and this model demonstrates that Ferragamo had designed shoes with circular decoration, either embroidered or painted in oils, from the beginning of the decade, even though the earliest examples cannot be found. This type of decoration is clearly related to trends in contemporary art, in particular to the "linear geometry" expounded by Venna in the Futurist *manifesto* of 1917.

15 'Iride' court shoe, 1935-1936

Length: 22 cm; heel: 8 cm
Label: Ferragamo's Creations. Florence Italy
Factory stamp: Hand Made in Italy
Series number, last, and size: F 835 510 4B

Upper formed of small circles embroidered silk thread in split stitch, joined together with bars in black Tavarnelle needlepoint lace. Toe cap, vamp edge, and insole edge cover in gold kid. Round toe. High heel in wood covered with gold kid. Gold kid sock. Leather sole.

One of the most widely publicized of Ferragamo's models, this shoe presents the ultimate version of the pull-over at the preceding number 14.

16 Laced shoe, 1936-1938

Length: 22.5 cm; heel: 8.5 cm
Label: Ferragamo's Creations. Florence Italy
Factory stamp: Made in Italy
Series number, last, and size: E 4231 710 4 1/2B

Four sets of eyelets. Upper in beige plaited bark with brown calf binding. Vamp and quarters decorated with brown-and-beige checked pattern. Brown calf tongue. Brown waxed lacing with brown calf tassels. Oval toe. High heel. Beige kid lining and sock. Leather sole.

17 Pull-over, 1936-1938

Length: 23 cm; heel: 7 cm

Prototype sandal. Upper formed of a wide band of natural hemp and plaited
cords of multicolored cotton. Plaited cotton cords form sling-back. High heel
with same decoration as upper.

18 Sandal, 1935-1938

Length: 23 cm; heel: 8.5 cm
Label: Ferragamo's Creations. Florence Italy
Factory stamp: Hand Made in Italy

Canvas upper, embroidered with squares in satin-stitched multicolored silk thread. Silver kid sling-back with metal buckle. High heel in wood covered with silver kid. Beige kid lining and sock with silver kid heel sock. Leather sole.

The patchwork upper of this sandal was a frequently seen element on Ferragamo shoes of this period. Here, the patchwork effect is created with embroidery.

19 Sandal, 1936-38

Length: 24 cm; heel: 9 cm
Label: Ferragamo's Creations. Florence Italy
Factory stamp: Hand Made in Italy
Series number, last, and size: NZ 235/3 DUX 5 1/2 C

Closed toe. Upper in woven grass from the Philippines, dyed various colors. Sling-back in plaited grass with tassels. Orange kid binding. Oval toe. High heel in wood covered with the same materials as upper. Orange kid insole edge cover. Beige kid lining and sock. Leather sole.

Campaigns encouraging the development of Italian national fashion had appeared in the Italian women's magazines 'Lidel 'and 'Popolo d'Italia' since the 1920s. Their purpose was to free Italian design from foreign influences by promoting local artisan traditions. The production of embroidery, lace, and other textiles in Italy increased as a result of these campaigns. Famous, indeed, were the lace of Burano, the embroidery of Orvieto, and the printed silks by Fortuny in Venice and Gallenga in Rome. The Fascist regime supported shows and presentations which accentuated Italian design. It favored the publication of Italian creations in the fashion press and urged women to buy national products. In 1932 the government established the Ente Autonomo per la Mostra Permanente Nazionale della Moda in Turin, later known as the Ente Moda. This organization monitored all sectors of the fashion industry, controlling production and reproduction of Italian designs. In 1935, a guarantee stamp was presented to companies producing goods both designed and manufactured in Italy. In 1939, The "Marca Oro" began to be presented to the designs which merited special recognition for their originality and quality. In 1936, Commentario Dizionario italiano della moda, a dictionary of fashion terms compiled by Cesare Meano, was published in order to purge the Italian fashion vocabulary of any foreign words. In accordance with this nationalist program, the term DUX was added to the information indicating the series, last, and size and to the labels of certain shoes manufactured during this period by Ferragamo.

20 Sandal, 1935-1936

Length: 22 cm; heel: 10 cm
Label: Ferragamo's Creations. Florence Italy
Factory stamp: Hand Made in Italy
Series number, last, and size: S 206 400 4B

Vamp composed of two strips of black satin and gold calf. Roman ankle strap in the same materials. Metal buckle. Mosaic of gilded glass glued to waxed canvas covers platform sole and cork wedge heel. Gold kid insole edge cover. Lining and sock in black satin. Leather sole.

The cork heel and platform sole of this model make it one of the first examples of the famous Ferragamo wedges, patented at the end of 1936 and immediately copied by other manufacturers. For many years, Ferragamo used a light, flexible layer of steel in the soles of his shoes instead of the leather reinforcements traditionally used by Italian shoemakers. The steel did not add weight to the shoes, which were famed for their lightness (only 120 grams instead of 250 gram weight of other shoes). At the outbreak of the Ethiopian war, importation of quality steel was forbidden in Italy. Since the steel available was of poor quality, Ferragamo turned to cork, which was already used for the heels of beach shoes. He pressed and glued a number of layers together, creating the famed yet initially reviled orthopedic wedge. The wedge shoe quickly became Ferragamo's most popular model, and was praised for the comfort of its sole, which provided the wearer with the sensation of walking on cushions.

21 Sandal, 1938

Length: 22 cm; heel: 13 cm
Label: Fortnum and Mason Ltd. Piccadilly W. Ferragamo's Creations.
Florence Italy
Factory stamp: Hand Made in Italy
Series number, last, and size: F 878 400 4B

Upper composed of padded gold kid straps, bordered with buttonhole stitch. Metal buckle. Platform sole and heel in layers of cork covered with suedes of various colors. Gold kid insole edge cover. Beige kid lining and sock with gold kid heel sock. Leather sole.

This much-publicized design was probably created for a famous client, possibly Judy Garland, though no documentation exists as proof of this shoe, Ferragamo seems to have been inspired by American film musicals, in which actresses often appeared swathed in glittering robes and precious furs on gilded pedestals, accentuating their star quality.

22 Sandal, 1938

Length: 22.5 cm; heel: 8 cm
Label: Ferragamo's Creations. Florence Italy
Factory stamp: Hand Made in Italy
Patent applied for

Upper formed of padded gold kid straps bordered with buttonhole stitch. Sling-back and instep strap in the same material. Metal buckle. Platform sole and wedge heel covered with black satin with hand-painted floral decoration. Wedge decorated with two vertical gold kid strips. Insole edge cover in gold kid. Black satin sock. Leather sole.

A March 1938 article in 'Per Voi Signora' mentions Oriental footwear as the inspiration for this type of high platform cork sole. Certainly the small groups of flowers painted on the wedge of this model are reminiscent of Chinese decorative motifs.

23 Sandal, 1938

Length: 22 cm; heel: 8 cm
Label: Ferragamo's Creations. Florence Italy
Factory stamp: Hand Made in Italy
Patent applied for
Series number, last, and size: O 155

Upper formed of two bands of gold and silver kid. Roman ankle strap. Metal
buckle. Cork platform sole and wedge covered with red velvet and decoration
in hand-embossed brass with strass. Gold kid insole edge cover. Purple satin
lining and sock. Leather sole.

A version of this model was first published in the May 1938 issue of 'Vogue'.
The name of the manufacturer was not given, but the magazine stated that the
shoes could be purchased at Saks for $100. In the September 1938 issue of
'Vogue', the model as shown was published as a Ferragamo design and tout-
ed as an "extravaganza" newly arrived in America from abroad. The original
model was created by Ferragamo for the Indian Princess, the Maharani of
Cooch Beahr.

24 Sandal, 1935-1936

Length: 21 cm; heel: 7 cm
Label: Ferragamo's Creations. Florence Italy
Factory stamp: Made in Italy
Series number, last, and size: 846 400 4B

Upper composed of red suede strips. Adjustable lacing over instep. Platform sole and wedge heel in wood with carved and painted geometrical decoration in yellow, blue, and red. Red suede insole edge cover. Beige kid lining and sock. Leather sole.

In addition to cork wedges, Ferragamo also experimented with wood for soles. To eliminate any excessive weight and to achieve greater flexibility, wedges were divided and sculpted.

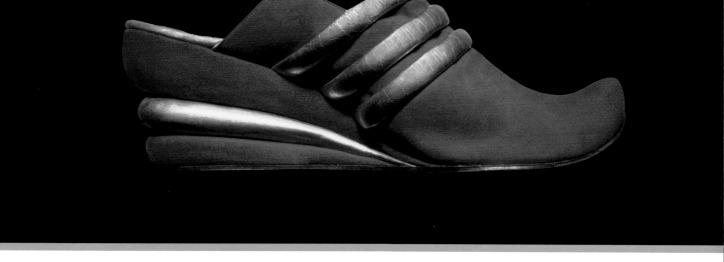

25 Mule, 1938

Length: 23 cm; heel: 3 cm
Label: Fatima Ferragamo's Creations. Florence Italy
Factory stamp: Hand Made in Italy
Series number, last, and size: AV 798 606 4iC

Pointed Oriental toe. Red suede upper with fringed vamp top lined with gold kid. Low heel in wood covered with red suede. Beige kid lining and sock. Leather sole.

There are many examples of Oriental toes in footwear designs of 1930s, especially at the end of the decade, when there was a movement toward more extravagant fashions. In September 1939, 'Vogue' published this model stating that it had been created by Ferragamo from a drawing by Oliver Messel for the English version of *The Thief of Baghdad*.

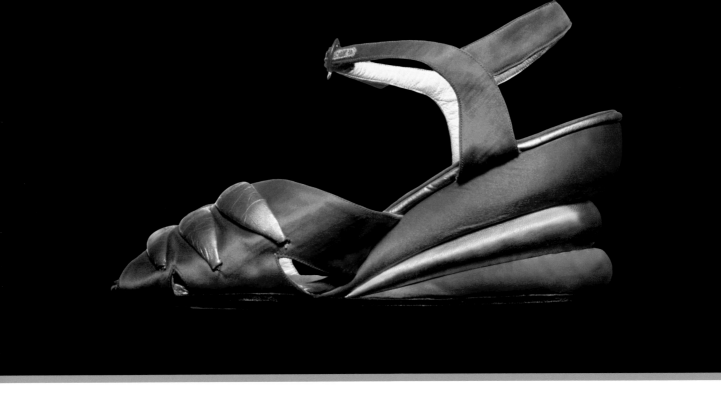

26 Sandal, 1936-1938

Length: 22 cm; heel: 7 cm
Label: Ferragamo's Creations. Florence Italy
Factory stamp: Hand Made in Italy
Patent applied for
Series number, last, and size: E 4240 400

Purple satin upper decorated at vamp center with three padded gold kid bows. Purple satin sling-back and instep strap reinforced with gold kid. Metal buckle. Wedge heel in three fluted layers of cork covered with purple satin and gold kid. Gold kid insole edge cover. Beige kid lining. Purple satin sock. Leather sole.

The search for new shoe forms characterized Ferragamo's designs of the mid-1930s. The rounded silhouette of the wedge, emphasized by the use of different materials and colors, echoes the decorative motif of the vamp. Apart from the aesthetic effect, the layered wedge of shaped cork required the skill of an experienced craftsman and two or three days work. The cork was rubbed down and pressed to ensure the stability of the sandal and correct fit.

27 Sandal, 1936-1938

Length: 23 cm; heel: 7 cm
Label: Ferragamo's Creations. Florence Italy
Factory stamp: Hand Made in Italy
Series number, last, and size: P 118 400 7787 50

Upper composed of bands and circles of gold kid perforated with two black satin bands. Ankle strap with same motif in black satin with black suede reinforcement. Metal and strass buckle. Wedge heel in three layers of cork covered with gold kid and black satin. Beige kid lining and black satin sock.

Ferragamo patented this wedge-heel model. It is probably one of the first examples of Ferragamo's orthopedic footwear.

28 Laced shoe, 1936-1938

Length: 22 cm; heel: 9.5 cm
Label: Ferragamo's Creations. Florence Italy
Series number, last, and size: E 4536 510 4 1/2 B

Four sets of eyelets. Layer of blue kid is cut and stitched and placed over layer of white kid for fish skin effect on vamp. Blue silk-cord lacing with blue and white kid tassels. Blue kid tongue. Round toe. Platform sole formed of three layers of cork covered alternately with blue and white kid. Beige kid lining and sock. Leather sole.

29 Laced shoe, 1941-1942

Length: 22 cm; heel: 7.5 cm
Label: Ferragamo Creazione. Firenze Italia
Factory stamp: Produzione Italiana

Four set of eyelets. Black woven cellophane upper. Black waxed lacing with tassels in red, yellow, and black kid. Oval toe. High heel in wood covered with black kid, which interlace at the waist. Beige kid sock. Leather sole.

"When wars break out and raw materials grow scarce it is always the high-grade industries which suffer first and hardest. War has no place for the best; it is the triumph of the shoddy. Top-class materials are not merely strictly rationed, they disappear entirely from the market; and the man whose quality of workmanship and business goodwill depend to a large extent upon the standard of his materials must fund adequate substitutes or shut down for the duration".

This was the dilemma facing Ferragamo in 1935, when sanctions were imposed on Italy by the League of Nations as a result of Mussolini's campaign in Ethiopia. The beginning of autarky necessarily led to a shortage of materials for the shoe industry.

"My first major problem was to find a substitute for the fine quality kid-skins which could be decorated in silver and gold for evening wear. I experimented with many materials but none were satisfactory. Then, one Saturday morning, I found the solution. My mother was extremely fond of chocolates, and this day I slipped across the road to the sweet shop and brought a box back to the house. As I unwrapped a chocolate for her I was attracted by its transparent paper wrapping. I turned the paper over in my hands. Here might be the substitute I was seeking. Tentatively I pulled at it and found it strong; then I pushed at it and found it weak – my finger went straight through…

Next day I went to the shop to buy not only chocolates for my mother but sheets of transparent paper for myself. I twisted them into thin ropes and experimented. Yes, they would serve. They gave the support and strength needed to the top of the shoes, and although the color was a pearly glow and not a pure silver gleam like the silver kid, it looked attractive. The thread gleamed through the paper with a translucent effect that was extraordinary pretty".

Cellophane uppers were also used on closed shoes. Cellophane is a plastic material derived from cellulose. Transparent, insoluble in water, and waterproof, it can be colored and printed. The fragile appearance of the material stands in contrast to its actual strength. Uppers in cellophane were lightweight, elastic, and allowed the foot to breathe.

30 'Spaghetti' sandal, 1938

Length: 22 cm; heel: 8 cm
Label: Ferragamo's Creations. Florence Italy
Factory stamp: Hand Made in Italy
Series number, last, and size: NZ 250 510 4B 2

Sandal with upper formed of interlaced suede strips in red, green, yellow, and blue. Sling-back with metal buckle. High heel in wood covered with red suede. Green suede insole edge cover. Beige kid lining and sock with yellow suede heel sock. Leather sole.

This amusingly named sandal was one of the most popular Ferragamo designs. Its success continued after the Second World War, when the model was revived. It was promoted in foreign newspapers and in advertisements for stores such as Lord and Taylor in New York.

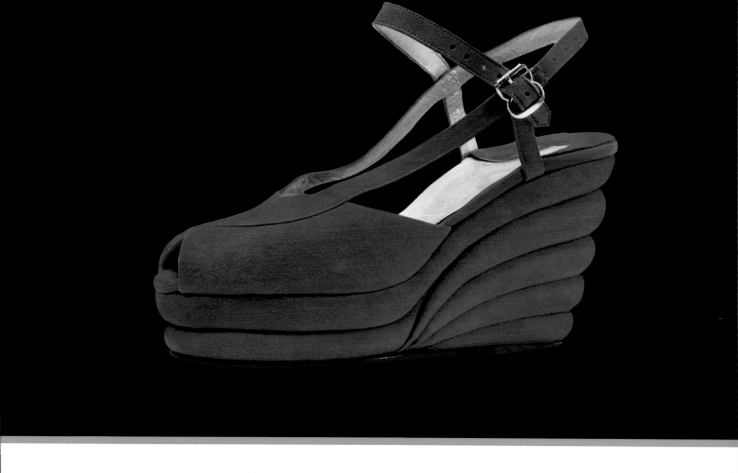

31 Sandal, 1942

Length: 21.5 cm; heel: 8 cm
Label: Ferragamo Creazione. Firenze Italia
Series number, last and size: E 4821 420 4 1/2 B

Vamp composed of two crossed bands of dark red suede which extend to form sling-back. Gilt-metal buckle. Suede insole edge cover. Platform sole and heel in layers of cork covered with red suede. Lining and sock in beige kid. Leather sole.

This sandal was made for the Brazilian singer and dancer Carmen Miranda.

32 Copy, 1938-1939

Length: 24 cm; heel: 13 cm
Label: Ferragamo Creazione. Firenze Italia
Factory stamp: Produzione Italiana Brevettato
Series number, last, and size: EFB 1087

Black velvet upper edged with silver kid. Sling-back formed of three strips of gold and silver kid. Metal buckle with strass. Wood "flat-through" sole (the heel is linked to the platform sole by a piece of wood) covered with silver kid. High heel covered with silver kid. Cork platform sole covered with alternating strips of silver and gold kid. Gold kid insole edge cover. Beige kid lining and sock with silver kid heel sock. Leather sole.

The original sandal was probably commissioned as part of a costume for a film or theater production, considering the originality of the design and the dramatic height of the platform sole. The design is reminiscent of the *chopine*, an incredibly high shoe worn in Venice and elsewhere in Italy during the Renaissance.

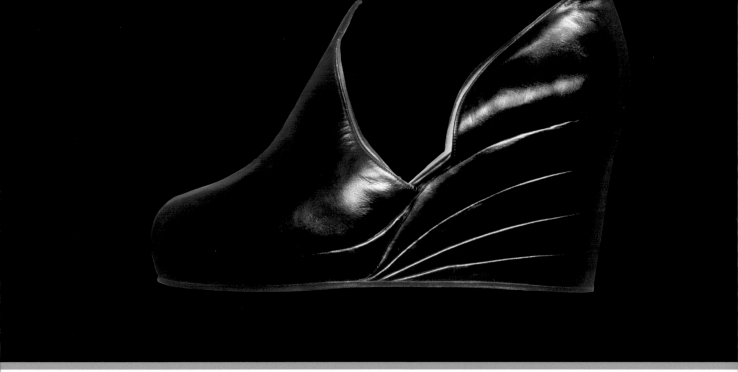

33 Black patent kid shoe, 1938-1939

Length: 23.5 cm; heel: 8 cm
Label: Ferragamo Creazione. Firenze Italia
Factory stamp: Produzione Italiana Brevettato
Series number, last, and size: BFB 1108/5 420 6 C

Two-piece upper. Vamp forms a point over instep. Pointed back. Round toe.
Platform sole and cork wedge heel covered with black patent kid. Beige kid
lining and sock. Leather sole.

34 Sandal, 1940

Length: 20 cm; heel: 6 cm
Label: Ferragamo's Creations. Florence Italy
Factory stamp: Hand Made in Italy

Vamp formed of two bands of black satin. Sling-back and instep strap in black satin. Metal buckle. Vertically fluted wedge heel and platform sole in cork covered with gold kid. Black satin insole edge cover. Beige kid lining and sole. Leather sole.

During the war years, the scarcity of quality materials stimulated the imagination of fashion designers. Ferragamo created many variations on the theme of the cork sole. The cork sole of this sandal, for instance, has been sculpturally modeled.

35 Sandal, 1941-1942

Length: 22 cm; heel: 7 cm
Label: Fortnum and Mason Ltd Piccadilly W Made in Italy;
Ferragamo's Creations. Florence Italy
Factory stamp: Made in Italy
Patent applied for

Closed toe. Black suede upper. V-shaped vamp with padded collar of gold kid.
Sling-back. Gold kid instep strap with same motif as vamp. Metal buckle.
Round toe. Square *cuneo* wedge heel in cork covered with black suede. Gold
kid insole edge cover continues to outline square back of wedge. Beige kid lining and sock with black suede heel sock. Leather sole.

This sandal, patented by Ferragamo and destined for the British market, was
designed for evening wear. The model was praised in 'Documento Moda's' summer 1942 issue for its simplicity of line and for the originality of the *cuneo* heel,
"elegantly profiled in gold". The shoe continued to be successful after the
Second World War.

36 Bordeaux suede shoe, 1942-1944

Length: 22.5 cm; heel: 5 cm
Label: Ferragamo's Creations. Florence Italy
Factory stamp: Made in Italy Brevettato
Series number, last and size: E 4303 444 4B

Vamp with tab, decorated with Bordeaux lizard and kid. Square back and toe.
Wedge heel in two layers of cork covered with kid and lizard. Beige kid lining
and sock. Welted leather sole.

37 Laced shoe, 1940

Length: 22 cm; heel: 7.5 cm
Label: Ferragamo's Creations. Florence Italy
Factory stamp: Made in Italy
Series number, last, and size: E 3450 4B

Two sets of eyelets. Black suede upper. Red kid strip extends from vamp center to decorate edge heel. Lacing in red kid. Black suede tongue. Round toe. Cork wedge heel covered with black suede and red kid. Beige kid lining and sock. Leather sole.

38 Ankle-boot sandal, 1944.

Length: 22 cm; heel: 8 cm
Label: Ferragamo Creazione. Firenze Italia

Open toe and heel. Upper of beige pilor (a cotton material similar to velvet) with brown grosgrain binding. Beige pilor tassels. Brown grosgrain insole edge cover. Beige kid lining and sock. Wedge heel in light blue painted wood.

39 'Ninfa' ankle boot, 1939

Length: 22 cm; heel: 8 cm
Label: Ferragamo's Creations. Florence Italy
Factory stamp: Made in Italy Brevettato
Series number, last, and size: CE 270/2 500 4B 87

Black suede. Six strips form pointed collar lined with purple satin on upper.
Oval toe. Cork wedge heel covered with black suede. Beige kid lining and
sock. Leather sole.

40 'Diva' sandal, 1940

Length: 23 cm; heel: 8 cm
Label: Ferragamo's Creations. Florence Italy
Factory stamp: Hand Made in Italy
Series number, last and size: SA 1484/1 DUX 4B

Upper composed of bands of sea-leopard skin in orange, blue, green, and yellow. Blue and orange sea-leopard skin, sling-back with metal buckle. Wedge heel in layers of cork covered with multicolored sea-leopard skin. Green sea-leopard skin insole edge cover. Beige kid lining and sock with yellow sea-leopard skin heel sock. Leather sole.

Salvatore Ferragamo had began to use sea-leopard skin for shoes in 1928, after his return from the United States. The fish skin was tanned and treated to attain a soft, supple texture. Since no tanning process had been discovered to eliminate the terrible smell of the fish skin, Ferragamo was forced to withdraw his designs from the market. Shortly before the Second World War, a German tanner managed to produce a fish skin for Ferragamo that was absolutely odor-free. During the war, however, this tanner was bombed, and it was not until 1954 that a Danish tanning firm managed to develop an odor-free skin, while also discovering a technique for dyeing it. This sandal was very popular in foreign markets, especially in the United States at the end of the forties, when Italian merchandise returned to the international marketplace.

41 Suede shoe, 1942-1944

Length: 23 cm; heel: 8 cm
Label: Farragamo Creazione. Firenze Italia
Factory stamp: Produzione Italiana Brevettato

Shoe with patchwork upper in square suede pieces in black, sea green, blue,
yellow, and rust. V-shaped vamp with binding in turquoise grosgrain. Oval toe.
Wedge heel in four layers of cork covered with strips of blue, yellow, rust, and
sea-green suede. Beige kid lining and sock. Leather sole.

42 Sandal, 1942-1944

Length: 23 cm; heel: 7.5 cm
Label: Ferragamo's Creations. Florence Italy
Factory stamp: Hand Made in Italy
Patent applied for
Series number, last and size: NZ 246 1 400 5B 1

Two-piece crocheted raffia upper in red, blue, yellow, orange, green, and natural stripes. Lacing in plaited multicolored raffia. Round toe. Wedge heel in pressed layers of cork glued together. Blue canvas insole edge cover. Beige kid sock. Leather sole.

43 'Molly' sandal, 1941-1942

Length: 23 cm; heel: 7 cm
Label: Ferragamo's Creations. Florence Italy
Factory stamp: Hand Made in Italy
Patent applied for
Series number, last and size: FA 970/1 1 4

Multicolored crocheted cellophane upper. Sling-back with metal buckle. Wedge heel formed of three layers of cork covered with strips of gold and silver kid. Silver kid insole edge cover. Beige kid sock with gold kid heel sock. Leather sole.

Some of the most popular patented models created by Salvatore Ferragamo during the period of national autarky were those made with cellophane. The transparent paper was plaited together like raffia. The 1942 summer edition of 'Documento Moda' included a photograph of this sandal with other cellophane models. Text accompanying the photograph stated that the robust nature of the material did not detract from "interesting aesthetic quality". The thin strips of transparent cellophane gave the shoe "an iridescent and almost crystalline quality; the colors woven together with an original and artistic sense".

44 Laced shoe, 1942-1944

Length: 23.5 cm; heel: 4.5 cm
Label: Ferragamo's Creations. Florence Italy
Factory stamp: Hand Made in Italy
Patent applied for
Series number, last and size: NZ 198 4141 1/2 B2

Four sets of eyelets. Woven multicolored raffia upper. Plaited raffia lacing with
tassels. Oval toe. Cork wedge heel covered with blue calf. Beige kid sock.
Leather sole.

45 Sandal, 1942-1944

Length: 21 cm; heel: 8.5 cm
Label: Ferragamo Creazione. Firenze Italia
Series number, last and size: EN 2598 42 B2

Two-piece blue suede upper. Sling-back with metal buckle. Wedge heel in pressed layers of cork, glued together, the bottom layer covered with blue suede. Beige kid lining and sock with blue suede heel sock. Sole in rubber derivative.

46 Sandal, 1942-1944

Length: 22 cm; heel: 7 cm
Label: Ferragamo Creazione. Firenze Italia
Series number, last and size: NZ 615 400 5 B 11

Black crocheted cellophane upper. Sling-back. Metal buckle. Wedge heel in three layers of cork covered with reptile skin. Black suede insole edge cover. Beige kid sock with black patent kid heel sock. Sole in rubber derivative.

The sole of this sandal is made from a rubber derivative obtained from the waste of natural or synthetic rubber through chemical, thermal, and mechanical processes. Other materials used for soles were Cuoital; Sapsa, produced by Pirelli, obtained from finely minced leather waste and rubber latex; Coriacel, produced in paper mills from leather, vegetable fibers, and glues; and *succedaneo*, made from the cuttings and shavings of the skins used by tanners and rubber latex paste.

47 Sandal, 1942-1944

Length: 23 cm; heel: 6 cm
Label: Ferragamo Creazione. Firenze Italia
Series number, last and size: N 28 5 1/2 B

Blue and white woven raffia upper. Sling-back with round blue button. Wedge heel in wood painted blue. Insole edge cover in blue grosgrain cloth. Beige waxed canvas sock. Open stitched and tacked Cuoital sole.

This sandal, destined for the German market, has a very rough sole, made from a defibered leather waste mixed with latex, called Cuoital. It was very difficult to work with (it often broke the shoemakers' needles and knives). The workmanship of this shoe does not match the refinement of other Ferragamo models. The name Ferragamo on the labels is presented in italics.

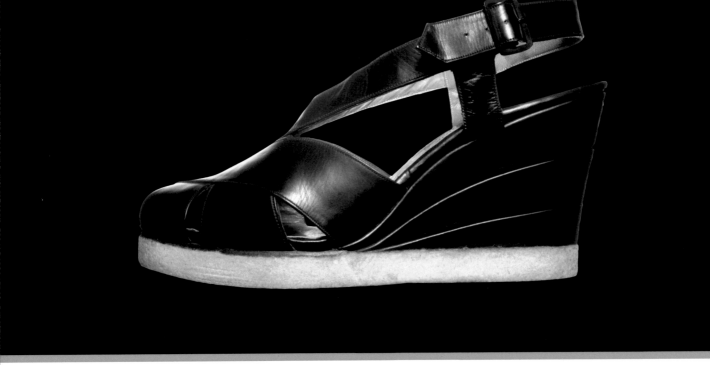

48 Sandal, 1942-1944

Length: 22 cm; heel: 6.5 cm
Label: Ferragamo Creazione. Firenze Italia
Series number, last and size: M 3308 420 4B

Upper composed of four bands of Bordeaux calf. Sling-back with metal buckle.
Wedge heel in three layers of cork covered with Bordeaux calf. Bordeaux calf
insole edge cover. Beige kid lining and sock with Bordeaux calf heel sock.
Open-stitched and tacked white felt sole.

49 Sandal, 1945-1947

Length: 23 cm; heel: 7 cm
Label: Ferragamo's Creations. Florence Italy
All Hand Made in Florence for Makanna Inc. Boston Mass.
Factory stamp: Hand Made in Italy
Series number, last and size: 1723 23 4B

Upper in alternating strips of black and white patent kid. High-cut vamp over instep. Roman ankle strap in the same materials. Wedge heel in three layers of cork covered with black and white patent kid. Black patent kid insole edge cover. Beige kid lining and sock with white kid heel sock. Leather sole.

The label indicates that this shoe model was made completely by hand and was destined for the American market. With the end of the war, Ferragamo once again began to export most of his production.

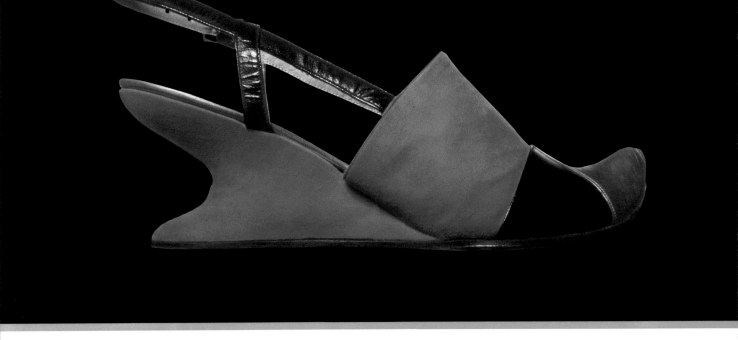

50 'Arabesca' sandal, 1944-1945

Length: 22.5 cm; heel: 6.5 cm
Label: Ferragamo's Creations. Florence Italy
Factory stamp: Hand Made in Italy Brevettato
Series number, last and size: CE 314 401 4B

Red suede upper. Black kid sling-back. Metal buckle. Pointed Orinetal toe in black and gold kid. F-shaped wedge heel in wood covered with red kid. Gold kid insole edge cover. Beige kid lining and sock. Leather sole.

In this sandal, the wedge is sculpted into and "F" shape. This was achieved by the joining of two pieces of elaborately hand-carved wood. This type of heel already existed in the United States, created by the industrial designer Seymour Troy, and published in 'Vogue' in 1939. This Ferragamo sandal, widely published in the years immediately after the Second World War, was featured in a spread on new shoes called *Back on the Road* in the November 1945 issue of 'Bellezza'.

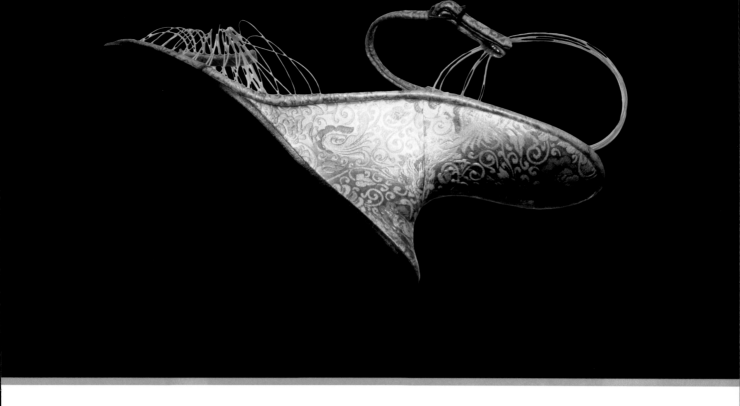

51 'Invisible' sandal, 1947

Length: 22.5 cm; heel: 8.5 cm
Label: Ferragamo's Creations. Florence Italy
Factory stamp: Hand Made in Italy Brevettato
Series number, last and size: CE 334 4b 510 s 155

Vamp formed of a single nylon thread passed repeatedly between each side of insole, perforating printed gold kid strip at center. Nylon sling-back repeats vamp motif. Printed gold kid instep strap with metal buckle. F-shaped wedge heel in gold kid. Printed gold kid insole edge cover. Beige kid sock. Leather sole.

The idea of using fishing line for the upper of the 'Invisible' shoe came to Ferragamo as he leaned out of a window in Palazzo Spini Feroni and watched men fish on the Arno River. The shoes, with their extraordinary, almost nonexistent appearance and dynamic form of the heel, a slimmer version of the classic cork wedge, were likened to the "chemical realization of ether" and to the work of Dalí in the press, as a representation of the renewed possibility to dream after the harsh reality of the war. The shoe was deemed revolutionary in an illustrated article in 'L'Europeo' on April 17, 1947. Not all the reviews of the shoe were so philosophical: an amusing article in the December 9, 1947 issue of 'Look' pointed out that the price of $29.75 for a pair of 'invisible' sandals would buy four tons of coal in a Europe that seemed more interested in flighty fashion than practical matters.

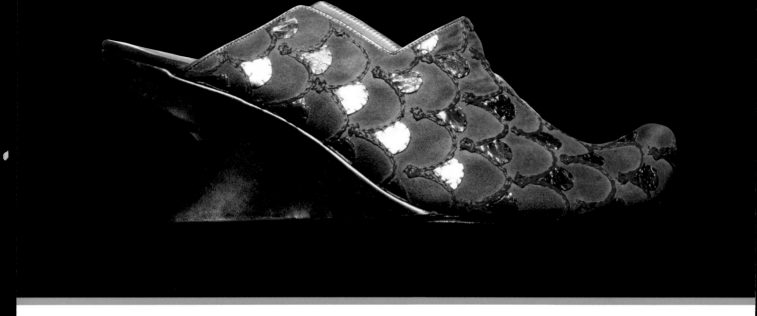

52 'Goccia' mule, 1948-1950

Length: 23.5 cm; heel: 6 cm
Label: Ferragamo's Creations. Florence Italy Brevettato
Factory stamp: Hand Made in Italy Brevettato
Series number, last and size: CE 336 401 4B

Powder-blue suede upper decorated with drop-shaped pieces of gold kid applied with open stitch, and with scallops embroidered in chain stitch with pink silk thread. Geometrically cut vamp edged with gold kid. Pointed Oriental toe. F-shaped wedge heel in wood covered with gold kid. Powder-blue suede insole edge cover. Beige kid lining and sock. Leather sole.

In the thirties, Ferragamo had designed mules with wedge heels and Turkish toes, inspired by Oriental footwear. At the beginning of the fifties, shoes with an upturned toe once again became fashionable. Perugia of France and Ferragamo of Italy both experimented widely with this particular style of footwear. In order to balance the increased length of the toe, the vamp tended to be higher on the neck of the foot, and the heels. Even the wedge, used for this model by Ferragamo, was given a characteristic curve, which did not, however, compromise the stability of the shoes nor the correct weight distribution of the body.

53 Sandal, 1947

Length: 22 cm; heel: 6 cm
Series number, last and size: CE 347/4 400 4B

Patchwork upper made of alternating rectangular pieces of blue, red, yellow, and green suede sewn together with open stitch in white calf. Red and blue suede sling-back with metal buckle. F-shaped wedge heel in wood, covered with red and blue suede. White calf insole edge cover. Beige kid lining and sock. Leather sole.

54 Sandal, 1948-1950

Length: 21 cm; heel: 8 cm
Label: Ferragamo's Creations. Florence Italy
Factory stamp: Hand Made in Italy
Series number, last and size: OS 805/5 588 4B

Pointed vamp in black crocodile. Open toe repeats vamp motif. Insole edge
and height heel in wood both covered with black crocodile. Beige kid lining
and sock. Leather sole.

Sandals remained the most popular summertime footwear styles throughout
the 1950s. Along with the traditional models with Greek lacing, new designs
consisted of an upper with either a closed or open toe, with no ankle strap.

55 Sandal with 'Kimo', 1951

Length: 22 cm; heel: 8 cm
Label: Ferragamo's Creations. Florence Italy
Factory stamp: Hand Made in Italy
Series number, last and size: OS 205 8 588 4B

High-cut vamp formed of interlacing gold kid strips. Insole edge and high heel in wood covered with gold kid. Beige kid sock. Leather sole. 'Kimo' sock in black silk.

In 1951, Ferragamo received the patent for a new type of women's shoe: a sandal with a gold kid or satin sock, called 'Kimo'. This two-part shoe immediately became fashionable: by simply changing the 'Kimo', the shoe could be adapted for either day or evening wear. As a "shoe for all occasions" it was warmly received by the press. A 1951 photograph shows Ferragamo with models wearing the new 'Kimo' sandals. This model was also used by Ferragamo, with clothes by Schubert, for the first Italian fashion show in Florence, on February, 12, 1951.

56 Court shoe, 1948-1950

Length: 22 cm; heel: 8 cm
Label: Ferragamo's Creations. Florence Italy
Factory stamp: Hand Made in Italy
Series number, last and size: AI 903 780 4 1/2 B

Black suede upper perforated on vamp and quarters with irregular strips of grey patent kid. Black grosgrain binding. Round toe. High curved Louis XV heel in wood covered with grey patent kid. Beige kid lining and sock. Leather sole.

57 'Oriana', 1949-1950

Length: 23 cm; heel: 8.5 cm
Label: Ferragamo's Creations. Florence Italy
Factory stamp: Made in Italy
Series number, last and size: ST 826 510 5B

Black suede upper. Vamp with envelope front. Round toe. High heel in wood covered with black suede. Beige kid and white lamb's wool lining and sock. Leather sole.

This was one of the shoes exhibited at the Italian stand at the "Europe Unite" exhibition held in London in 1950. The model was also produced for Harvey Nichols of Knightsbridge, a famous London department store.

58 Black suede shoe, 1950-1952

Length: 23 cm; heel: 4.3 cm
Label: Ferragamo's Creations. Florence Italy
Factory stamp: Hand Made in Italy
Patent Pending
Series number, last and size: MK 304 4180 6 1/2 B 5

One-piece upper. Stitched vamp top-line. Thin black suede strip at vamp center with lateral buckle in metal. Slightly raised toe. Arch and medium round heel in wood covered with black suede. Beige kid lining and sock. Leather forepart sole and top-piece.

In 1950 Ferragamo began to use a method of construction for uppers in which only one seamless piece of leather was employed. This type of construction was called an 'Aquila' and required three feet of leather for each pair of shoes. The model was also worn by Claudette Colbert.

59 'Fiammetta' laced shoe, 1948-1950

Length: 22.5 cm; heel: 4.5 cm
Label: Pompeian Designed by Ferragamo. Florence Italy
Factory stamp: Hand Made in Italy
Series number, last and size: 247 6AA

Three sets of eyelets. Blue and natural woven raffia upper with checked pattern. Blue kid binding. Blue and natural plaited raffia lacing with tassels. Medium heel in wood covered with blue kid. Beige kid sock. Leather sole.

60 Sandal, 1949-1950

Length: 22 cm; heel: 7.5 cm
Label: Ferragamo's Creations. Florence Italy
Factory stamp: Hand Made in Italy

Closed toe. Bordeaux crocodile vamp and instep strap with metal buckle.
Round toe. Insole edge and high heel in wood, both covered with Bordeaux
crocodile. Beige kid lining and sock. Leather sole.

61 'Campia' mule, 1949-1950

Length: 22 cm; heel: 4 cm
Label: Ferragamo's Creations. Florence Italy
Factory stamp: Hand Made in Italy
Series number, last and size: CA 11 4148 4 1/2 B

Light brown ostrich skin upper. Vamp divided laterally by brown calf strip. Four sets of eyelets. Ostrich skin tongue. Brown calf binding. Round toe. Low heel in wood covered with light brown ostrich skin. Ostrich skin insole edge cover. Beige kid lining and sock. Leather sole.

62 'Ranina' sandal, 1950-1952

Length: 22 cm; heel: 8.5 cm
Label: Ferragamo's Creations. Florence Italy
Factory stamp: Made in Italy
Series number, last and size: M 022 588 4 1/2 B

Closed toe. Upper in black Tavarnelle needlepoint lace with floral designs and decorated with black sequins. Black satin collar and sling-back. Metal buckle. Oval toe. High Louis XV heel in wood and insole edge both covered with black satin. Transparent vinyl lining. Beige kid sock with black satin heel sock. Leather sole.

The model was created for the Italian actress Anna Magnani.

63 Sandal, 1950-1952

Length: 23.5 cm; heel: 19 cm
Label: Ferragamo's Creations. Florence Italy
Factory stamp: Hand Made in Italy
Series number, last and size: CS 1694 519 S 5 1/2 B

Closed toe. Net upper in white Tavarnelle needlepoint lace, decorated with gold and white sequins. V-shaped vamp with gold kid collar. Sling-back and instep strap in gold kid. Metal buckle. Round toe. High, thin heel in wood covered with geometric patterns in strass. White kid insole edge cover. Beige kid lining and sock with gold kid heel sock. Leather sole.

Major innovations in footwear fashion of the thirties were to be found in the design and decoration of heels. They were offered in high and slender, stiletto, low and square, bobbin, facet, comma-shaped, and polygonal styles, incorporating ornate rhinestone, plastic, wood, metal, and ceramic elements.

64 'Vitrea' sandal, 1952-1954

Length: 25 cm; heel: 10 cm
Label: Ferragamo's Creations. Florence Italy
Factory stamp: Hand Made in Italy

Sandal in vinyl, decorated with little pearls in pink glass and topaz-colored glass beads forming circular patterns and borders. Gold kid sling-back. Metal buckle. High tapered heel in wood covered with gold kid. Pink kid insole edge cover. Beige kid lining and sock with gold kid heel sock. Leather sole.

Synthetic resins, such as vinyl, had been widely used in footwear design since 1928. An article in the December 21, 1946 issue of 'Footwear News' explained: "They (resins) are made by combining salt, natural gas, coke, and limestone to produce vinyl compounds that are suitable for shoe materials. The converter, or manufacturer, buys these resins from the raw material manufacturer, and combines them with plasticizers, pigments, stabilizers, and lubricants to make a plastic mass. This is kneaded thoroughly, squeezed several times between heated colanders to mix thoroughly and form a uniform surface, dried and run off in rolls.
This is the plastic sheeting that is used for soles, uppers, and other parts of a shoe. The high-gloss patent finish so particularly successful in plastic sheeting is produced by press polishing. Vinyl plastic sheetings offer both utility and style possibilities. They are extremely resistant to abrasion, moisture, oil, grease, and alcohol and can be made transparent, translucent, or opaque in pastel or bright colors".

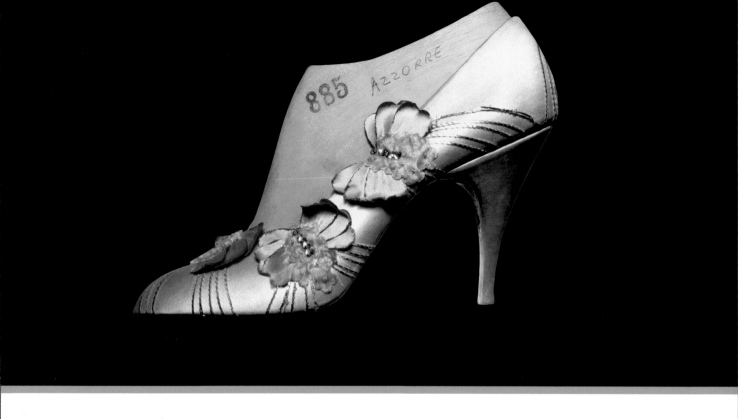

65 'Azzorre' pull-over, 1955-1956

Prototype court shoe. White satin upper decorated with pink silk and silver thread. Vamp edge decorated with butterflies made of pink satin, white peluche, yellow strass, and beads. Pointed toe. High stiletto heel in wood covered with satin.

66 Court shoe, 1955-1956

Length: 22 cm; heel: 9 cm
Label: Ferragamo's Creations. Florence Italy
Factory stamp: Brevettato Hand Made in Italy
Series number, last and size: 46 A 1114

Upper in brown suede, Vamp edge embroidered in brown silk. Round toe.
High heel covered in bronze mica. Beige kid lining and sock. Gloved arch in
brown suede. Leather colored forepart shoe.

Although heels with brass and gilt copper inlaid with stones and strass did not
originate with Ferragamo, in 1955 he patented some exciting innovations. The
first was a heel in red, bronze, and green, given a metallic finish with a shiny
thin layer of mica, an ortho and metaldehyde silicate of aluminium with alka-
line metals.

67 'Damigella' pull-over, 1955-1956.

Length: 23 cm: heel: 9 cm

Prototype short boot. Elasticized white silk with gold brocade effects forms ruched collar with gold edging on upper. Pointed toe. Stiletto heel in wood covered with gold kid.

The model was created for the Italian actress Sophia Loren.

68 Sandal, 1955

Length: 23 cm; heel: 9 cm
Label: Ferragamo's Creations. Florence Italy
Factory stamp: Hand Made in Italy
Patent Pending

Closed toe and uppers in green and gold silk brocade with floral designs. Vamp bordered with two gold kid strips forms a knot at center. Gold kid sling-back with metal buckle. High stiletto heel covered in brilliant green mica. Insole edge and arch covered in gold kid. Beige satin lining and sock. Forepart sole in transparent vinyl. Leather top-piece.

The vinyl sole created a window through which it was possible to see the bottom of the wearer's foot when she sat down and crossed her legs.

69 Sandal, 1955-1956

Length: 25 cm; heel: 9 cm
Label: Ferragamo's Creations. Florence Italy
Factory stamp: Hand Made in Italy
Series number, last and size: DAK 1424 885 7 AA 1

Closed toe. Embroidered vamp with floral designs in satin stitched multicolored silk thread, colored glass pearls, and strass joined with bars of ivory Tavarnelle needlepoint lace. Vamp collar and sling-back in gold kid. Metal buckle. Pointed toe. High stiletto heel in wood and insole edge both covered with gold kid. Beige kid lining and sock with gold kid sock. Leather insole.

The model was created for the Italian actress Sophia Loren.

70 'Cassandra' sandal, 1955-1956

Length: 22 cm; heel: 9 cm
Label: Ferragamo's Creations. Florence Italy
Factory stamp: Hand Made in Italy Brevettato

Vamp formed of three black satin strips, which interlace at center. Sling-back with metal buckle. High stiletto heel covered with satin and decorated with strass. Insole edge and arch covered with black satin. Black satin sock. Leather forepart sole and top-piece.

71 Sandal, 1956

Length: 22 cm; heel: 8.5 cm
Label: Ferragamo's Creations. Florence Italy
Factory stamp: Hand Made in Italy
Series number, last and size: AL 1706 5805 5B

Upper formed of piece of cloth entirely covered in Venetian glass beads and strass with an asymmetrical strap in gold kid to the heel. Metal buckle. Insole edge cover in gold kid. Brass heel decorated in inlaid polychrome strass. Beige kid lining and sock with heel sock in beige kid. Leather sole.

72 Ballerina shoe, 1954

Length: 23,5 cm; heel: 1 cm
Label: Ferragamo's Creations. Florence Italy
Factory stamp: Hand Made in Italy Brevettato
Series number, last and size: VA 559 6B 812

Black suede upper and kid strip closed by buckle. Low oval heel and shell sole derived from Indian sole opanke.

The model was created for Audrey Hepburn.

73 Sandal, 1954-1955

Length: 24 cm; heel: 1 cm
Label: Pompeian Designed by Ferragamo. Florence Italy
Factory stamp: Hand Made in Italy

Upper formed of semicircular band in orange pontova, reinforced with black patent kid band. Low heel in two layers of black patent leather. Black patent kid insole edge cover. Beige kid lining and sock. Leather sole.

Pontova is a type of synthetic raffia. It was crocheted for use in Pompeian model uppers throughout the fifties.

74 'Claretta' sandal, 1952-1954

Length: 24 cm; heel: 8.5 cm
Label: Pompeian Designed by Ferragamo. Florence Italy
Factory stamp: Hand Made in Italy
Series number, last, and sizes : AK 639 588 6B 2

Vamp formed of two semicircular pieces in brown pontova, divided laterally by brown calf strip gathered on vamp front. Brown kid sling-back with metal buckle. High heel in wood and insole edge both covered with calf. Beige kid lining and sock. Leather sole.

75 Court shoe, 1956

Length: 24 cm; heel: 11 cm
Label: Ferragamo's Creations. Florence Italy
Factory stamp: Hand Made in Italy
Series number, last, and sizes: PE 1395 7 1/2 B

Gold kid upper. Pointed toe. Stiletto heel covered in kid. Beige kid sock and lining with suede heel sock. Leather sole.

These shoes, created for Marilyn Monroe in Joshua Logan's film *Bus Stop,* were purchased at the auction of Marilyn Monroe's personal effects at Christie's in New York on October 28, 1999.

76 Court shoe, 1958-1959

Length: 24.5 cm; heel: 11 cm
Label: Ferragamo's Creations. Florence Italy
Factory stamp: Hand Made in Italy
Series number, last, and sizes : FS 502 A PE.1154 899 7 1/2 B

Upper in black suede with small black calf appliqués. Pointed toe. Stiletto heel. White kid sock and lining. Leather sole.

These shoes created for Marilyn Monroe were purchased at the auction of Marilyn Monroe's personal effects at Christe's in New York on October 28, 1999.

77 Court shoe, 1959-1960

Length: 24 cm; heel: 11 cm
Label: Ferragamo's Creations. Florence Italy
Factory stamp: Hand Made in Italy
Series number, last and size: PE 428 708 3391 7 1/2 B

Upper in black suede with decorative elongated oval cuts lined in fuchsia kid.
Pointed toe. Fuchsia kid sock and lining. Leather sole.

These shoes were purchased at the auction of Marilyn Monroe's personal
effects at Christie's in New York on October 28, 1999.

78 Court shoe, 1958-1959

Length: 23.5 cm; heel: 10.3 cm
Label: Ferragamo's Creations. Florence Italy
Factory stamp: Hand Made in Italy
Series number, last, and sizes: Art, 733 F 3991

Yellow suede upper perforated with five holes bordered with thin kid strips in Bordeaux, blue, pale blue, pink, black, white, and violet. Low-cut vamp with Bordeaux calf binding. Pointed toe. High stiletto heel in wood and metal covered with yellow suede decorated at upper. Beige kid lining and sock. Leather sole with reinforced arch.

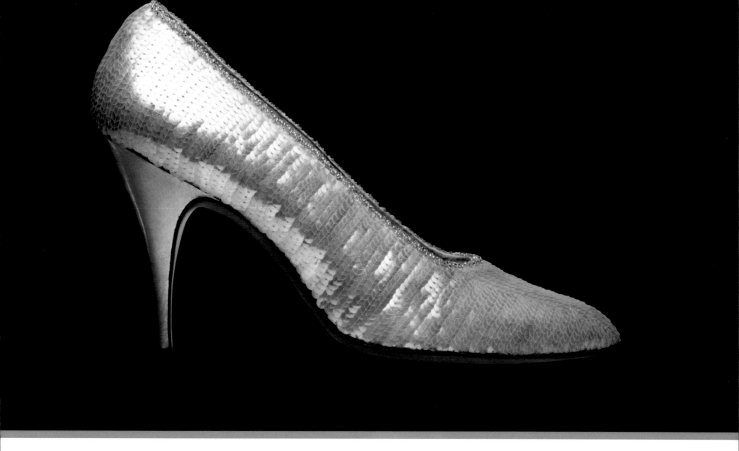

79 Court shoe, 1958

Length: 23.5 cm; heel: 10 cm
Label: Ferragamo's Creations. Florence Italy
Factory stamp: Hand Made in Italy
Series number, last, and sizes: INJ 757 885 6 1/2 B

Evening sole with cloth upper entirely covered in iridescent sequins. Vamp edge decorated with gilt Venetian glass beads. Pointed toe. Stiletto heel in wood with steel reinforcement covered in gold kid. Beige kid lining and sock. Leather sole.

80 Pull-over, 1961

Heel: 9 cm

Upper in white satin trimmed with black feathers and strass. High heel covered in satin.

The model was made for the wife of an American tycoon.

CHRONOLOGY | BIBLIOGRAPHY

CHRONOLOGY

1898 Salvatore Ferragamo was born on June 5th, in Bonito in the province of Avellino, the eleventh of the fourteen children of Maria Antonia and Antonio Ferragamo.
Left Italy for the United States and worked a short spell at the Queen Quality Shoe Manufacturing Company in Boston.

1919 In Santa Barbara, he opened a shoe repair and shoemaking shop that would soon become famous. Studied anatomy at the University of California and started to work for the motion picture industry.

1920 Capitalized on his studies of the anatomy of the foot by patenting a system for putting fractured limbs in traction.

1923 Moved to Hollywood and opened the Hollywood Boot Shop, frequented by movie stars.
Returned to Italy and settled in Florence, where he opened a factory in the outskirts (Via Mannelli 54).

1930 Lucio Venna, the Italian painter and exponent of the Futurist movement, produced the first advertisement for Ferragamo and designed the label that would appear on the inside of his shoes.

1933 Forced to declare bankruptcy and close down his business following the dollar crisis. Rented rooms in the historic Palazzo Spini Feroni in the heart of the city.
Back in business again, he patented the first shoe with a wedge heel, his most famous invention.

1938 On the ascendant, he bought Palazzo Spini Feroni, which has been the company's headquarters ever since.

New shops opened in London (Bond Street) and Rome (Via Condotti).

Exports to the USA continued.

1939 Married on November 9th to Wanda Miletti, daughter of the doctor and mayor of Bonito, who was to give him six children (Fiamma, Giovanna, Ferruccio, Fulvia, Leonardo, and Massimo).

1947 After the war, he received the Neiman Marcus Award (the fashion Oscar) for his 'invisible' sandal made of nylon fishing line.

Made shoes for Elsa Schiaparelli and Christian Dior fashion shows in Florence.

1950 His milestone trip to the Far East led to the first exports to Japan.

1951 Took part in the first Italian fashion show, in Palazzo Torrigiani, with the famous 'kimo' sandal for Emilio Schubert's collection.

1955 Patented leopard seal skin (first in Denmark then in the rest of Europe). Sophia Loren was the witness at the launch of the product at the Grand Hotel in Rome.

1957 Salvatore Ferragamo's autobiography published in London, in English.

1958 Began partially mechanical production of footwear with the Ferrina Shoes and Ferragamo Debs lines.

1960 Died on August 7th, in Ronchi, a seaside resort near Florence.

BIBLIOGRAPHY

ASCHENGREEN, K., S. Ricci and G. Vergani (eds.), *I protagonisti della moda Salvatore Ferragamo (1898-1960),* exhibition catalogue (Palazzo Strozzi, Florence, 4 May-30 June 1985), Florence, 1985.

_____, S. Ricci and G. Vergani (eds.), *Salvatore Ferragamo: The Art of the Shoe 1927-1960*, exhibition catalogue (Victoria and Albert Museum, London, 31 October 1987-7 February 1988), Florence, 1987.

ASPESI, N., *Il lusso e l'autarchia. Storia dell'eleganza italiana*, Milan, 1982.

BOSONI, G., F.Picchi, M. Strina and N. Zanardi, *Original patents of Italian design 1946-1965*, Milan, 2003.

"Coloured Spot-lights for Your Summer", in 'Vogue', 1 May 1938, pp.86-87.

FERRAGAMO, S., *Shoemaker of Dreams*, London, 1957.

FIDOLINI, M., *Dal Secondo Futurismo al Cartellone Pubblicitario: Lucio Venna*, Bologna, 1987.

"Fine Italian Hand for Shoes", in 'Vogue', 15 July 1937, pp. 59 and 88.

"Light on your feet", in 'Vogue', 1 October 1938, p.122.

MALOSSI G. (ed.), *La Sala Bianca: nascita della Moda Italiana*, exhibition catalogue (Palazzo Strozzi, Florence, 25 June-25 September 1992), Milan, 1992.

RICCI, S., *Materials and creativity*, exhibition catalogue (Museo Salvatore Ferragamo, Florence), Florence, 1997.

_____, (ed.), *Salvatore Ferragamo: The Art of the Shoe*, exhibition catalogue (County Museum, Los Angeles 1992), New York 1992.

_____, *Shoes and famous feet*, exhibition catalogue (Museo Salvatore Ferragamo, Florence), Milan 2000.

_____, *Ideas, models, inventions*, exhibition catalogue (Museo Salvatore Ferragamo, Florence), Livorno, 2004.

Salvatore Ferragamo with one of his shoemakers, 1955. Photo Locchi. Locchi Historical Archive, Florence.

Mercedes Iturbe
Director, Museo del Palacio de Bellas Artes

Stefania Ricci
Director, Museo Salvatore Ferragamo

Catalogue and Exhibition Curators
Mercedes Iturbe and Stefania Ricci

Exhibition Design
RBA

Installation and Production
Melaverde

Film Editing
Videocast

Communication and Press
Ernesto Martínez

Public Relations
Anke Buller
Letizia Campana
Aideé Cortés

Thanks to the following for their support:
El Palacio de Hierro
Grey Goose
HSBC
Mercedes-Benz

CONSEJO NACIONAL PARA LA CULTURA Y LAS ARTES

Sari Bermúdez

President

INSTITUTO NACIONAL DE BELLAS ARTES

Saúl Juárez

General Director

Daniel Leyva

Fine Arts Division

Gabriela López

Visual Arts Division

Mercedes Iturbe

Director, Museo del Palacio de Bellas Artes

Patricia Pineda

Public Relations

MUSEO DEL PALACIO DE BELLAS ARTES

Director

Mercedes Iturbe

Assistant Director

Guadalupe García

Administration

José de Jesús Campos

Exhibition Coordination

Gabriela Gil

Cataloguing and Control of Works

Tannia Lozano

Design and Museography

Juan Manuel Garibay

Communications

Ernesto Martínez

Public Relations

Aideé Cortés

Educational Services

Tere Hidalgo

§ § § § § § § § § § § § § § § § §
§ § § § § Walking Dreams § § § § §
§ § Salvatore Ferragamo 1898-1960 § §
was printed in March 2006 by Artes
Gráficas Palermo in Madrid, Spain § Three
thousand six hundred copies were printed on
170-gram Consort Royal silk bluewhite paper § § § § § § Set in typefaces
of the families Bauer Bodoni, Helvetica Neue, Interstate, and Filosofia
§ § § § § § § § Mexico City § § § § § § § § § § § § § § § MMVI § §
§ § § § § § § § § § § § § § §   § § § § § §